CONTENTS

CHAPTER ONE	An Introduction to the Working Time Regulations 1998	1
CHAPTER TWO	The 48-Hour Working Week	13
CHAPTER THREE	Rest Periods	31
CHAPTER FOUR	Night Workers	43
CHAPTER FIVE	Holiday Entitlement	61
CHAPTER SIX	Young Workers	71
CHAPTER SEVEN	Enforcement and Remedies	81

CHAPTER 1

An introduction to the Working Time Regulations 1998

1. When In Force?

The Working Time Regulations 1998 (SI 1998/1833) (the Regulations) became law in England, Wales and Scotland on 1st October 1998. There are separate, but equivalent, regulations applicable to Northern Ireland (The Working Time Regulations (Northern Ireland) 1998 SR No. 386), which came into force on 23rd November 1998.

With effect from these dates, employers have been required to comply with legal obligations to restrict and monitor their workers' working time. Equally, "workers" (a broader definition than "employees"), have new rights and entitlements to maximum working weeks and to rests and breaks.

To enforce these obligations, rights and entitlements, the Regulations are a hybrid of health and safety duties – enforceable by the criminal law – and enhanced employment protection rights – enforceable in employment tribunals.

2. About this Guide

This Guide outlines the obligations, rights and entitlements contained within the Regulations, explains the circumstances in which they apply and gives practical information and advice for both employers and workers on how to comply. Although a useful reference, it should not be considered as a substitute for legal advice in individual circumstances. The Regulations are new law and there are many unanswered questions; at the time of writing, there has been only two reported cases and more court and employment tribunal decisions are inevitable. Gradually, these decisions will help clarify the Regulations, in particular the scope of the definitions and the flexible circumstances in which some of the obligations, rights and entitlements can be modified, or even excluded. Given their European origin, European law interpretation and European Court judgements will also be of fundamental importance.

3. European Origin

3.1 The Directives

The Regulations derive from the European Union and are designed to implement the provisions of the EC Working Time Directive (No.93/104/EC) and certain parts of the EC Young Workers Directive (No.94/33/EC).

The Working Time Directive (the Directive) was introduced as part of the Social Charter, the EU initiative designed to focus on the Social Union, rather than simply the traditional ecomonic union envisaged by the common market. The Directive was adopted by all member states on 23rd November 1993, giving member states three years, i.e. to 23rd November 1996, to implement some of the principal provisions of the Directive into their national laws.

Article 1 states the purpose and scope of the Directive, confirming that the Directive lays down minimum safety and health requirements for the organisation of working time and applies to:

(a) minimum periods of daily rest, weekly rest and annual leave, to breaks and maximum weekly working time; and

(b) certain aspects of night work, shift work and patterns of work.

The Directive is also stated to apply to all sectors of activity, both public and private, with the exception of workers engaged in the sectors of air, rail, road, sea, inland waterway and lake transport, sea fishing and other work at sea, and the activities of doctors in training.

3.2 The UK Challenge

Although only a qualified majority vote in favour was necessary to adopt the Directive, the UK abstained from the vote, claiming that its legal basis was defective. This was because the Directive was adopted under Article 118a of the Treaty of Rome. Article 118a provides that the EC Council of Ministers shall adopt, by means of directives, minimum requirements for encouraging improvements, especially in the working environment, to ensure a better level of protection of the safety and health of workers. The UK Government claimed, however, that the Directive was essentially a social policy measure, which should have been created under Article 100. The purpose of Article 100 is to harmonise legislation affecting the establishment or function of the common market and which covers provisions relating to the rights and interests of employees. More importantly, Article 100 requires unanimous approval, in which case the UK would have been able to veto the measure.

The UK's second argument was on the basis of Article 235, which is used as the legal foundation for measures where no other provision of the Treaty of Rome applies. Again, Article 235 requires unanimous approval. The UK also argued that the Directive constituted a breach of the principle of proportionality, because it went beyond the minimum requirements permitted under Article 118a.

The UK launched a legal challenge in the European Court of Justice (ECJ), seeking to have the Directive declared invalid. The case took three years to be decided, during which time the UK Government took no steps to introduce the Directive into UK Law. The ECJ finally gave judgment on 12th November 1996, a mere 11 days before some of the Directive's principal provisions were due to be law in the UK.

3.3 The ECJ Ruling

The ECJ ruled that the Directive had been properly adopted under Article 118a with one minor exception. The Directive originally provided that the minimum weekly rest period must in principle be a Sunday. The Court ruled that this provision should be annulled, as there was no reason why Sunday was more closely connected with health and safety than any other day.

On the proportionality point, the Court ruled that it must first be ascertained whether the means which were employed were suitable for the purpose of achieving the desired objective and whether they went beyond what was necessary to achieve it. The Court concluded that the objective of harmonising national legislation on health and safety, while maintaining improvements made could not be achieved by measures less restrictive than those in the Directive. There was therefore no breach of the principle of proportionality.

4. The Young Workers Directive

The Young Workers Directive was also adopted under Article 118a of the Treaty of Rome on 22nd June 1994. This Directive required implementation within two years and the UK has implemented the various parts of it in four different sets of regulations. The Regulations implement various provisions of the Directive which restrict the working time of adolescent workers, i.e. those above minimum school leaving age but under 18. The application of the Regulations to young workers is explained in detail in Chapter 6.

5. Implementation in the UK

5.1 Consultation

Following the ECJ ruling, the then Conservative Government issued a consultation document in December 1996, which demonstrated clearly an intention to interpret the Directive as narrowly as possible, and to comply only with the minimum requirements.

On 8th April 1998, the new Labour Government issued a further consultation document, this time with draft regulations attached. This document supported the approach of maximum flexibility, making use of the wide range of derogations available within the Directive, whilst promoting fair minimum standards and measures to ensure the proper protection of workers from risks to their health and safety. The Consultation Paper stated: "'The Directive' will provide protection to the most vulnerable employees against working excessive hours and will give them a right to the sorts of entitlements, in terms of rest breaks, rest periods from work and paid annual leave, enjoyed by the majority of workers in the UK."

5.2 The Regulations

The finalised Regulations were published on 30th July 1998 and came into force on 1st October 1998.

5.3 Regulatory Guidance

On 2nd September 1998 the DTI published Regulatory Guidance, detailing how the Government believes the Regulations should be interpreted and applied.

The DTI Guidance has no legal status. The law is contained within the Regulations and the Directive, from which they are derived. The DTI Guidance will, however, be referred to by employers, workers and their representatives, in seeking to interpret the Regulations and will clearly be influential. References to the DTI Guidance are made throughout this book.

6. Interpretation of the Regulations

6.1 EC Law Principles

When considering the meaning of the Regulations, the EC law principles applicable to interpreting UK legislation derived from directives should be borne in mind.

There are three basic principles:

(a) UK courts and employment tribunals will, wherever possible, interpret the Regulations "purposively", so as to give effect to the terms of and purpose of the Directive;

(b) workers employed by the state or "an emanation of the state" may be able to rely directly on the provisions of the Directive, if the Regulations are not adequate to give full effect to the terms of the Directive. For this to happen, however, the relevant term of the Directive must be sufficiently clear, precise and unambiguous, to be applied without the need for implementing legislation;

(c) workers may be able to bring claims for damages against the UK Government, if they suffer loss in consequence of a failure by the Government to properly implement the Directive. These claims are known as "Francovich" claims, named after the ECJ case which decided this principle.

6.2 Definitions

There are a number of key definitions which are vital to understanding how the Regulations are designed to work and these crop up throughout the Regulations and of course the chapters of this Guide. It is therefore useful to preview these terms now.

6.3 Who is a "Worker"?

The Regulations apply wholly or in part to "workers" from all sectors save for the excluded sectors (see Part 6.5 below). "Worker" is defined in Regulation 2(1) as follows:

"'Worker' means an individual who has entered into or works under (or where the employment has ceased, worked under) –

(a) a contract of employment; or

(b) any other contract, whether express or implied and (if it is express) whether oral or in writing, whereby the individual undertakes to do or perform personally any work or services for another party to the contract whose status is not by virtue of the contract that of a client or customer of any profession or business undertaking carried on by the individual;

and any reference to a worker's contract shall be construed accordingly."

The definition covers not only employees, but is broader in scope. However, the genuinely self-employed (i.e. those who carry out business activities on their own accounts) are expressly excluded from the Regulations.

The Regulations also apply to the "special classes of person" provided for in Part V of the Regulations. These include:

(a) agency workers, not otherwise classified as "workers", who are supplied by an agent to work for another party (see Regulation 36);

(b) those in Crown employment, i.e. those who work for a Government department or public body (see Regulation 37);

(c) members of the armed forces (see Regulation 38);

(d) House of Commons and House of Lords staff (see Regulations 39 & 40);

(e) persons holding the office of police constable or an appointment as a police cadet (see Regulation 41);

(f) non-employed trainees, i.e. those receiving relevant training otherwise than under a contract of employment; the person undertaking the training will be regarded as the employer (see Regulation 42); and

(g) agricultural workers, subject to various modifications concerning annual leave entitlements, which are set out in Schedule 2 (see Regulation 43).

Of particular relevance to employers generally is the first special class, agency workers. This class applies to individuals supplied by one person (the agent) to do work for another (the principal) under a contract or arrangement made between the agent and the principal, but who are not otherwise "workers" (i.e. because they do not themselves have a contract with either the agent or the principal, and are not genuinely self-employed). Those who contract to provide a service through their own businesses are excluded. An example of this would be information technology contractors operating through their own limited companies, but obtaining work through agencies.

However, secretaries, administrators and other individuals engaged by companies through employment agencies will be covered by the Regulations. The party responsible for paying these workers will be deemed to be the employer for the purposes of the Regulations. This will usually be the agency. To comply with its obligations, therefore, the agency will need to rely to a certain extent on co-operation by the principal, in terms of effective time recording and rest break provision. Agencies cannot "contract out" of their obligations but may seek to demonstrate that they have taken reasonable steps to comply with their duties, by imposing contractual obligations upon the principal. This is unlikely to be sufficient alone, given the purpose of the Regulations to safeguard health and safety, and agencies will need to put in place systems to monitor the working arrangements operated by their clients (the principals) and act upon reports of non compliance from their workers, in order to safeguard their positions.

6.4 Who is a Young Worker?

Regulation 2(1) defines these as workers who are over the minimum school leaving age but under the age of 18 (see Chapter 6).

6.5 Excluded Workers

The Directive specifically excludes certain sectors and the Regulations follow suit.

The following activities are excluded:

(a) the air, rail, road, sea, inland waterway and lake transport sectors, sea fishing and other work at sea;

(b)   doctors in training (the DTI Guidance clarifies this to cover the NHS training grades; pre-registration house officer, house officer, senior house officer, registrar, senior registrar and specialist registrar). The European Commission is however planning to provide similar protection for the above workers in the near future; and

(c)   specified services, such as the armed forces or the police, or to certain specific activities in the civil protection services (e.g., the fire and ambulance services), whose characteristics inevitably conflict with the provisions of the Regulations. The Guidance states it is up to such services to identify the activities which conflict.

Whether or not a worker falls within one of these exclusions will ultimately be a question for the courts or employment tribunals. Particular questions have arisen in relation to the transport sector. Are workers providing a transport function ancillary to their employers' main businesses excluded? It would appear to make little sense to exclude those who work for distribution companies and not those who undertake distribution for a supermarket employer for example. Arguably both are excluded, and this view is supported by the Guidance.

The DTI Guidance does give some further assistance. The Guidance states: *"employers will need to consider whether the particular workers fall within a sector or not. The location of the work, for example a port, railway station or airport will not necessarily mean that those doing it are excluded. Furthermore, neither will workers involved in the movement of goods or people to or from a mode of transport (for example, in docks or loading/unloading onto/from road vehicles) necessarily be excluded. Where workers are directly involved in the operation of the sector, such as baggage handlers and signal and maintenance staff they are more likely to be excluded from the Regulations but where they are not (e.g. construction workers at an airport) the exclusion is not likely to apply"*.

Further workers are excluded from various provisions of the Regulations by derogations, for example workers whose time is "unmeasured" and certain family and domestic workers. The scope of these derogations and how they apply to each of the Regulations' provisions, are explained in following chapters.

6.6 What is "Working Time"?

The basic effect of the Regulations is to divide time between what is "working time" and what is not (be it rest periods, annual leave or other rest time).

Regulation 2(1) defines "working time" as follows:

"'Working time', in relation to a worker, means –

(a) *any period during which he is working, at his employer's disposal and carrying out his activities or duties;*

(b) *any period during which he is receiving relevant training; and*

(c) *any additional period which is to be treated as working time for the purpose of these Regulations under a relevant agreement;*

and 'work' shall be construed accordingly."

Working time may, or may not, happen to coincide with the time for which a worker receives pay, or with the time during which the worker is required to work under the terms of his/her employment contract.

Where (b) and (c) above do not apply, whether the time is "working time" will depend on all three elements of the definition in (a) being satisfied. The DTI Guidance recognises that there may be uncertainty in a number of situations, for example whether a worker's mere presence at a workplace, for example during a lunch break, or when "on call" constitutes working time. This question is explored in more detail in Chapter 2 . Ultimately, however, it will be for the courts and employment tribunals to decide whether time is working time in the individual circumstances of each case.

The Regulations, however, do allow for workers and employers to make a "relevant agreement", to clarify what constitutes rest periods and what constitutes working time at their own workplace. Such an agreement might, for example, confirm that all contractual time counts as working time, even where it includes rest breaks or periods spent away from the workers' place of work.

6.7 Relevant Agreements

The Regulations allow employers and workers to agree how specific provisions of the Regulations should apply to their own workplaces. Agreements regarding what time should be included in the definition of working time is one such example. However, agreements can also be entered into to modify the Regulations and even to exclude certain of the basic entitlements in certain circumstances.

The Regulations refer to three types of agreement; a "relevant agreement", a "workforce agreement" and a "collective agreement".

"Relevant agreement" is a term which encompasses both:

(a) a workforce agreement applying to the worker in question;

(b) any provision of a collective agreement forming part of a worker's contract of employment; or

(c) "any other agreement in writing which is legally enforceable between the worker and his employer".

Relevant agreements therefore include workforce agreements and collective agreements, as well as other written agreements, the most obvious of which is the worker's written contract of employment.

A "collective agreement" is one entered into between the employer or employer's association(s) and one or more of the recognised trade unions, within the meaning of Section 178 of the Trade Union and Labour Relations (Consolidation) Act 1992.

"Workforce agreements" are agreements made between employers and elected representatives of their workers, in circumstances where those workers are not covered by a collective agreement(s). This is a new concept which allows employers in non-unionised workplaces to make valid agreements with representatives of the workforce. However, Schedule 1 of the Regulations sets out the conditions and requirements which must be satisfied for such an agreement to be valid.

6.8 Rules for Workforce Agreements

To be valid, the agreement must:

(a) be in writing;

(b) have effect for a specified period not exceeding five years;

(c) apply to all relevant members of the workforce, or to all relevant members of the workforce who belong to a particular group (i.e. a specified unit or department);

(d) be signed by either the representatives of the workforce, or the representatives of the particular group to which the agreement applies, as appropriate. Alternatively, if there are fewer than 20 employees on the date on which the agreement is first available for signature, it should be signed either by the appropriate representatives or by the majority of the workers employed;

(e) before making the agreement available for signature, the employer must provide a copy of the text of the agreement to all workers to whom it is intended to apply and such guidance as those workers reasonably require in order to fully understand the terms of the agreement.

The representatives referred to must be "duly elected", and for this purpose all the requirements listed in Paragraph 3 of Schedule 1 must be satisfied. These requirements are as follows:

(a) the employer must determine the number of representatives to be elected;

(b) the candidates for election must be relevant members of the workforce, and the candidates for election as representatives of a particular group (for example, workers within a particular department or unit or performing a particular function) must be members of that group;

(c) no eligible worker is unreasonably excluded from standing for election;

(d) all relevant members of the workforce are entitled to vote for representatives of the workforce, and all members of a particular group are entitled to vote for representatives of that group;

(e) workers can vote for as many candidates as there are representatives to be elected;

(f) the election is conducted so as to ensure that, so far as is reasonably practicable, those who vote do so in secret and the votes given at the election are fairly and accurately counted.

It should also be noted that representatives have the right not to suffer dismissal or detriment as a result of standing for election or acting as a representative under the Regulations (see Chapter 7 – Enforcement and Remedies).

CHAPTER 2

The 48-hour working week

1. The Requirement and the Employer's Duty

The Regulations provide that a worker's working time, including overtime, shall not exceed an average of 48 hours per week (Regulation 4(1)). This is a mandatory requirement, which applies to all contracts of employment, unless the individual worker has "opted out" (see below). The averaging period to be applied (known as the "reference period"), however, varies depending on the circumstances (see part 6 below).

Where a worker's working time exceeds this average, the effect of this mandatory requirement is to give the worker (unless he/she has opted out) the right to refuse to continue working until his/her average working hours meet the requirement. Workers have the right to seek a declaration from the courts to this effect, which is what happened in the recent case of *Barber and others -v- R J B Mining UK Ltd,* High Court (Queen's Bench Division) 3, March 1999.

In addition, Regulation 4(2) imposes a duty on every employer to take *"all reasonable steps, in keeping with the need to protect the health and safety of workers, to ensure that"* average weekly working time does not exceed 48 hours.

This duty, in common with other health and safety duties, is enforceable by either the local authority or health and safety executive ultimately by way of prosecution in the Magistrates Court or the Crown Court. The maximum fine is £5,000 in the Magistrates Court and is unlimited in the Crown Court. (See Chapter 7 – Enforcement and Remedies).

To avoid committing offences under this section, employers need to be able to demonstrate that they have taken all reasonable steps to ensure the limit was complied with. This will entail developing a system to keep an on-going and accurate record of working hours. In turn, this will help to identify those at risk of over working and enable consideration to be given to alternative working arrangements which comply with the limits. These could include, for example, the reorganisation or reallocation of work. The other option is to seek individual opt-out agreements from the workers concerned.

In summary, therefore, individual workers have the right not to work in excess of the average 48-hour limit (unless they opt out); where they do work in excess of this requirement, their employer may be prosecuted. Workers who opt out may work in excess of the average 48-hour limit, subject to their entitlements to rest breaks and paid holiday and to special protection for night workers (see Chapters 3, 4 and 5).

2. Who is Covered?

All "workers" are covered, save for the exclusions explained below. The Regulations define "worker" as follows:

"'Worker' means an individual who has entered into or works under (or, where the employment has ceased, worked under) –

> (a) *a contract of employment; or*
>
> (b) *any other contract, whether express or implied and (if it is express) whether oral or in writing, whereby the individual undertakes to do or perform personally any work or services for another party to the contract whose status is not by virtue of the contract that of a client or customer of any profession or business undertaking carried on by the individual;*

and any reference to a worker's contract shall be construed accordingly."

It is important to appreciate that this definition is broader than "employee". Essentially all workers (including all employees (full, part-time, temporary and casual employees), other temporary workers and freelancers) are covered, save for the genuinely self-employed. The genuinely self-employed are those who pursue a business activity on their own account and will usually be paid by invoice rather than by a wage packet. They are also likely to be in the position to decide whether to take on the work, how to do it and to perform similar work for any number of other customers.

The Regulations also apply to workers supplied by employment agencies. However, the genuinely self-employed operating their own limited companies but obtaining work through agencies (for example, information technology contractors), will remain excluded. Otherwise, individuals engaged by companies through an employment agency will be protected by the Working Time Regulations. In the absence of a contract between the worker and either the agency or the agency's client, the employer for the purposes of the Regulations will be whoever is responsible for paying the worker. In most employment agency arrangements, therefore, it will be the agency who will be responsible for that worker under the Working Time Regulations.

On a practical basis, this will require agencies to review their contracts and working arrangements with their customers, to ensure that there are sufficient safeguards in place to comply with the limit. The agency will need to be in a position to establish that it has taken "all reasonable steps" to ensure compliance and this is likely to involve more than simply transferring responsibility contractually to the client, and include an element of monitoring, etc. Given the usual pay structure, however, keeping records of the hours worked will usually be straightforward.

The other implication, of course, is that the cost of engaging a worker through an employment agency is likely to increase, particularly given the increased rights of such workers to, for example, paid annual holiday (see Chapter 5).

3. Who is Excluded?

All "workers" (as explained above) benefit from the average 48-hour maximum working week, except:

- (a) those excluded from the Working Time Regulations altogether, i.e. transport sectors, doctors in training, the armed forces and the civil protection services (see Chapter 1 Part 6.5);

- (b) workers employed as domestic servants in a private household (i.e. au pairs, nannies, etc.);

- (c) those whose working time is "unmeasured"; and

- (d) those individuals who specifically opt out of the protection.

4. Whose Working Time is "Unmeasured"?

Regulation 20 provides that the average 48-hour maximum does not apply to workers where *"on account of the specific characteristics of the activity in which he is engaged, the duration of his working time is not measured or predetermined or can be determined by the worker himself"*. Examples given are:

(a) managing executives or other persons with autonomous decision, taking powers; and

(b) family workers, i.e. those working in the family business; and

(c) workers officiating at religious ceremonies in churches and religious communities.

These are examples only. Any worker whose job meets this description could qualify. This is a matter of interpretation and the Department of Trade and Industry Guidance provides a helping hand. From the Guidance, it is clear that the most important issue is one of control. To be excluded, such workers will have a very high degree of control over the hours they work and their time will not be monitored or determined by their employers. The Guidance states *"such a situation may occur if a worker can decide when the work is to be done, or may adjust the time worked as they see fit. An indicator may be if the worker has discretion over whether to work or not on a given day without needing to consult their employer".*

The last phrase may turn out to be crucial. How many employees can honestly say they have the discretion not to turn up on the Monday and to work on Saturday instead? Certain company directors may fall within this category, but managers at a lower level are unlikely to in the normal course of events. But seniority is not in itself an essential characteristic – it is the activity which is important. Sales staff may equally be excluded if they are given an area to service and the discretion to plan their routes as they see fit. If the employer judges by results and the employee has complete discretion when to make the calls, his/her working time is likely to be unmeasured.

Many contracts include a clause setting out the employee's normal working hours on Monday to Friday, but adding that "the employee will work such additional hours as may be necessary to ensure the proper performance of his/her duties". This is unlikely to be sufficient to render that worker's working time unmeasured. The contract confirms the minimum number of hours, over which a worker may have no discretion, before adding for good measure the additional hours which may be required. There may not, therefore, be the necessary degree of control.

5. What is "Working Time"?

5.1 The Basic Definition

In assessing whether or not the average 48-hour limit is being observed, it is clearly crucial to appreciate what time counts towards that limit and what does not.

The basic definition of working time within the Regulations is in three parts and is stated to mean *"(a) any period during which he is working, at his employer's disposal and carrying out his activities or duties."*

All three elements of this definition need to be satisfied before the time is classified as "working time".

The definition then goes on to confirm that working time also includes *"(b) any period during which [the worker] is receiving relevant training, and (c) any additional period which is to be treated as working time for the purposes of these Regulations under a relevant agreement"*.

5.2 Travel Time

Since all three elements need to be satisfied to meet the basic definition under (a) above, some activities naturally related to work will not count as working time. Consider travel: travel to and from work will not meet any of the three elements, but travel to and from a business meeting may well do. If the worker's duties include travel to visit customers, then when en route he/she is working, at the employer's disposal and carrying out activities or duties. This is likely to remain the position where a worker travels direct from home to a business meeting and vice versa.

5.3 "On-Call" Time

"On-call" time is another case in point. When on call, a worker does not work or carry out activities or duties, unless and until the pager vibrates or the phone rings to summon the worker into work. Time spent at home or out with friends in the interim would not therefore count as working time.

Taking this one step further, if the worker is on call at his/her place of work, the Guidance suggests that if the worker sleeps on the premises, or is otherwise at leisure, such time would not count as working time, since the worker would not be working.

5.4 Break Times

Break times such as the lunch hour may or may not be working time depending on how the worker spends them. A meeting scheduled at lunchtime will be working time. This may have a knock-on implication for the rest break entitlement (see Chapter 3). Those workers whose 20-minute minimum break per working day of six hours or more is scheduled at lunchtime (which is invariably the case for office workers), will be entitled to take the break at another point of the day, if they are required to work through lunch.

A lunchtime spent at leisure, however, would clearly not constitute working time.

5.5 Home Working

The Guidance also mentions home working, stating *"where a worker took work home, time worked would only count as working time where work was performed on a basis previously agreed with the employer"*.

So if a worker decides to take work home for a day (for example to complete a particular project without disturbance) that would be working time, provided he/she has the agreement of the employer. However, a Sunday morning spent working under the worker's own steam to catch up or to try to get ahead, would not constitute working time. Although carrying out activities or duties which may otherwise be performed during normal working hours, the worker would not be at the employer's disposal.

5.6 Agreements

Grey areas will of course arise as the Regulations are applied in practice and case law develops. This could be where section (c) of the Regulations' definition becomes important. Section (c) gives the parties to a relevant agreement the ability to agree what additional time (i.e. over and above time falling within the basic three-part definition and training) constitutes working time. So in some workplaces where time is spent "on-call", waiting for that call could be agreed to be working time. Also, the questions of travel time and break times could be clarified to each party's satisfaction.

In this context, "relevant agreement" means either a workforce agreement (i.e. a collective type agreement but between the employer and non-trade union employee representatives), a collective agreement (between the employer and a recognised trade union) or any other agreement legally enforceable between the employer and the worker, such as a contract of employment.

6. How is the 48-Hour Limit Measured?

6.1 Basic 17-Week Reference Period

The 48-hour maximum is an average maximum and the standard averaging period is 17 weeks. The Regulations refer to this as the reference period. Unless a relevant agreement provides for successive 17-week blocks, for example 1st January to 30th April, followed by 1st May to 28th August and so on, the limits must be met during any period of 17 weeks.

This could be significant for workers whose workloads fluctuate. Take for example retail staff who need to perform considerable overtime in the run up to Christmas and throughout the January sales. If successive periods are agreed in a relevant agreement, this could work well. For example there could be one period from 3rd September to 31st December followed by the next period from 1st January to 30th April. Provided the working time is lower during the first part of the September to December reference period, increased hours over and above 48 hours per week during December may not mean that the 48-hour maximum will be exceeded on average overall. The extra time worked in January would be included in the next reference period, which could then be evened out between February and April.

If successive periods have not been agreed, however, the 48-hour maximum would need to be complied with during any period of 17 weeks. This could result in the working time for both December and January being assessed in the same reference period.

The 17-week reference period is a basic starting point and the following variations should be noted.

6.2 New Workers

The reference period for workers employed for less than 17 weeks is the period elapsed since he/she started work. So, if a worker has been employed for six weeks, during those six weeks the worker must not have worked for more than 48 hours per week on average at any point.

Since the maximum limit must be met at any time during the period elapsed since day one of the job, the worker cannot be required to work 60 hours for the first three weeks on the basis that only 36 hours per week will be required for the next three. The worker can however work 36 hours for each of the first three weeks and 60 hours during each of the next three weeks because, this way round, the maximum is not breached at any point. See also Part 6.3 below.

This provision is a safeguard for temporary and casual staff, who may be drafted in to cover periods of peak demand.

6.3   26 Weeks

The reference period for workers falling within the more flexible categories specified by Regulation 21 is 26 weeks instead of 17 weeks. For these categories, the average weekly working hours of new workers must not exceed 48 hours at any time during the first 26 weeks of employment.

6.4   Up to 52 Weeks

A reference period of any length of up to 52 weeks can in some circumstances be agreed in relation to particular workers, or groups of workers, under a collective or workforce agreement, as appropriate.

The circumstances in which this is allowed are where there are *"objective or technical reasons or reasons concerning the organisation of work"* (Regulation 23(b)). This phrase is not defined, nor does the Guidance elaborate. However, it is thought sufficiently widely drawn to encompass annualised/banked hours, arrangements predominant in the manufacturing industry, to accommodate flexible shift patterns.

What should be noted is that such an increased reference period can only be agreed for workers, or for a particular group of workers, by a collective or workforce agreement. Provisions within individual contracts of employment will not be sufficient. Employers currently operating annualised arrangements under individual contracts, therefore, will need to consider whether – in order to comply with the average 48-hour maximum – a collective or workforce agreement needs to be negotiated to confirm the arrangements. Without such an agreement, the basic 17-week reference period (or the 26-week one if the Regulation 21 special circumstances are relevant) will apply.

If a collective or workforce agreement cannot be negotiated, such employers should consider negotiating individual written opt outs of the 48-hour protection (see Part 9 below). Conversely, a total opt out of the 48-hour protection can only be achieved with the written agreement of each individual employee. Collective or workforce agreements cannot be used to achieve opt-outs.

An increased reference period of up to 52 weeks can be agreed via collective or workforce agreement (as appropriate), to replace the basic 17-week period for all staff, both existing and new recruits. For new recruits, however, the basic effect is the same as with the 17 or 26-week periods; no more than 48 hours can be worked on average during any part of that initial reference period. Where hours fluctuate, therefore, the shorter working hours must come first.

6.5 Special Circumstances (Regulation 21)

Regulation 21 sets out the whole range of circumstances in which a 26-week reference period applies, in substitution for the basic period of 17 weeks. These circumstances are also relevant elsewhere in the Regulations because they confer increased flexibility in terms of night work, rest breaks and the daily and weekly rest provisions (see Chapters 3 and 4).

The circumstances are, in the main, formulated as descriptions and examples, rather than a specific or exhaustive list. There is therefore considerable room for interpretation, and this is recognised by the Guidance. So, the reference period may be extended to 26 weeks:

(a) *"where the worker's activities are such that his place of work and place of residence are distant from one another or his different places of work are distant from one another"*. The Guidance suggests that this may apply to workers where, because of the distance from home, it is desirable for them to work longer hours for a shorter period to complete the task more quickly or, where continual changes in the location of the work make it impracticable, to set a pattern of work.

(b) *"where the worker is engaged in security and surveillance activities requiring a permanent presence in order to protect property and persons, as may be the case for security guards and caretakers or security firms"*.

(c) *"where the worker's activities involve the need for continuity of service or production, as may be the case in relation to –*

   (i) services relating to the reception, treatment or care provided by hospitals or similar establishments, residential institutions and prisons;

   (ii) work at docks or airports;

   (iii) press, radio, television, cinematographic production, postal and telecommunications services and civil protection services;

   (iv) gas, water and electricity production, transmission and distribution, household refuse collection and incineration;

   (v) industries in which work cannot be interrupted on technical grounds;

   (vi) research and development activities;

   (vii) agriculture."

These are examples listed from the original EU Working Time Directive and are not exhaustive. Other circumstances involving the need for continuity of service or production may well also be covered, provided that they fall within the spirit of the Directive. European legislation is interpreted purposively, i.e. in line with the purpose the legislation is designed to achieve. The purpose is clear – primarily to protect the health and safety of workers – but also (as the Government explained in its consultation paper) to promote family life by safeguarding social and family time. Thus a commercial decision to work around the clock would not justify the adoption of the 26-week reference period unless there is also a technical reason why the machinery needs to be kept running. Without this further reason, an increase on the basic 17-week reference period would need to be agreed by virtue of a collective or workforce agreement. Alternatively, the individual workers could agree to opt out of the 48-hour maximum protection altogether (see Part 9 below).

(d) *"where there is a foreseeable surge of activity, as may be the case in relation to –*

    (i)   agriculture;

    (ii)   tourism; and

    (iii)   postal services."

Again, these are examples only. It is likely that retail staff working increased hours over Christmas and New Year would also be subject to the 26-week reference period. Equally, the description may apply to other categories working to foreseeable deadlines. Accounts staff who work increased hours just before the financial year ends, for example, or tax or financial advisers in the immediate run up to the new tax year. In all such cases, it will be a matter of fact and degree whether the circumstances fit the description in the light of the aims of the Directive.

The final circumstances are in –

(e) *"where the worker's activities are affected by –*

    (i)   an occurrence due to unusual and unforeseeable circumstances, beyond the control of the worker's employer;

    (ii)   exceptional events, the consequences of which could not have been avoided despite the exercise of all due care by the employer; or

    (iii)   an accident or the imminent risk of an accident."

This category essentially covers emergencies beyond the employer's control.

In relation to each of the above special circumstances, the Guidance says that it is up to each employer to take a view as to whether the relevant conditions are satisfied for each individual worker's situation. Until there is case law to explain the parameters of these circumstances, there will be an element of uncertainty.

Collective and workforce agreements to agree extended reference periods, may therefore prove popular, particularly in workplaces where that culture is already established. There are examples throughout the Regulations of the potential flexibility provided by such agreements, and employers who are used to negotiating personal contracts on an individual basis may wish to explore whether such agreements could work advantageously for them. Otherwise, the best advice is to take a common sense interpretation to the special circumstances and to apply them within the spirit of the Regulations. The more "stretched" the interpretation, however ingenious, the greater the likelihood of a challenge!

7. Calculation of the 48-Hour Average

The average weekly working time is calculated by dividing the total actual "working time" during the appropriate reference period, by the number of weeks in that reference period.

Note the contrast between actual working time in this context, and the normal hours of work referred to in Regulation 6 in the context of "nightwork". This can lead to the odd situation where the worker does considerable voluntary overtime. The voluntary overtime is clearly working time and is included within the 48-hour calculation, but it is not included within the calculation of average nightwork, since nightwork is based on "normal working hours".

Periods during which the worker is absent on holiday, on sick leave or maternity leave, and periods during which the worker has opted out of the 48-hour protection altogether, must be taken into consideration, to ensure an accurate calculation of the average working time. These are known as "excluded days". To facilitate this, Regulation 4(6) provides the formula as follows:

$$\frac{A + B}{C}$$

"where –

A is the aggregate number of hours comprised in the worker's working time during the course of the reference period;

B is the aggregate number of hours comprised in his working time during the course of the period beginning immediately after the end of the reference period and ending when the number of days in that subsequent period on which he has worked equals the number of excluded days during the reference period; and

C is the number of weeks in the reference period".

In short, therefore, to ensure an accurate average, you need to make up the number of excluded days during each reference period by the equivalent number of working days from the next reference period.

For example, if S works for 630 hours during a reference period running from 1st January to 30th April, during which S also has two weeks' holiday, the employer must include the first two working weeks from the next reference period within the calculation to obtain the correct average. If S's working time during these next two weeks is 85 hours, the calculation is therefore:

$$630 + 85 \div 17 = 42 \text{ hours}$$

In this case, therefore the 48 hour average maximum has been complied with.

The two working weeks taken from the next reference period are also included in the calculation of the average over the next reference period.

8. Workers With More Than One Job

Employers should note that the provisions of regulations 4 (1) and 4 (2) are not restricted to one job. Where a worker has more than one job, the average 48-hour maximum working week applies across both jobs. Given the health and safety purpose of the Regulations, this interpretation does make sense, but can give rise to practical difficulties.

The DTI Guidance recognises the employers' obligations in these circumstances, stating:

"Employers are required to take all reasonable steps to ensure that workers do not exceed an average of 48 hours of weekly working time. Such steps would include enquiring whether the worker was working elsewhere (or requesting that they be notified on a worker getting other work) and, if they were, adjusting working arrangements accordingly."

The problem with the suggestion that working arrangements should be adjusted accordingly is how and in favour of whom? If an office worker has an evening bar job and has not opted out, which employer needs to adjust or risk committing a criminal offence, or risk the worker exercising his/her right not to work more than the 48-hour maximum per week?

To help resolve these issues, employers should bring the obligations under the Regulations to the attention of all their workers, and seek to identify those who should consider opting out of the Regulations. This is explored further in Part 9 below. In addition, for new employees, employers should consider including a new provision within contracts of employment to the effect that workers agree not to obtain work elsewhere during their current employment, without the written permission of their employer. Conditions of such permission should then be that the worker enters into an opt-out agreement, in respect of the 48-hour working week, if the new job would render this necessary, and gives the employer full details of the additional hours worked in the second job. This would be necessary to comply with the record-keeping requirements (see Part 10 below).

A similar procedure can be used to sanction voluntary overtime, i.e. an employer would permit the worker to volunteer for extra work, provided an opt-out was in place if need be.

9. The Opt-Out

9.1 The Agreement

If the length of reference period is insufficient to result in an average of 48 hours or less per week, the employer must either alter working arrangements to keep to the limit or negotiate individual opt-out agreements. The Directive permits member states, including the UK, to provide for opt-out agreements until November 2003, at which point opt-out agreements will no longer be permitted

An opt-out agreement:

(a) must be between the individual worker and the employer; they cannot be negotiated collectively;

(b) must be in writing;

(c) may relate to a specified period or apply indefinitely; and

(d) must be terminable by the worker by at least seven days' but no more than three months' notice.

9.2 New Workers

Apart from these requirements, there is no magic form of opt-out agreement. For new employees, the contract of employment is one obvious place to include an opt-out agreement. This gives rise to the question of what to do if a new recruit objects to the opt-out agreement and refuses to the sign the contract including that provision. Strictly speaking, only "workers" are protected by the Regulations. A prospective recruit who has yet to accept the contract and has yet to start work is not technically a worker. A word of caution, however, for those tempted to withdraw the offer of the contract at that point. A purposive interpretation of the Regulations might stretch to including such individuals within the definition of worker, giving them protection against detrimental treatment. Furthermore, a well-advised individual might simply start work and give immediate notice of termination of the opt-out.

9.3 Existing Workers

For existing workers, the position is potentially more complex. Employers should consider whether the opt out is really necessary to comply with their duty. In most cases, the averaging period will ensure that the maximum is not exceeded on average.

There are two further reasons for thinking carefully before requesting opt outs. Firstly, the record-keeping requirements for those who have opted out are more onerous on the employer (see Part 10 below). Secondly, there is the risk of creating a two-tier workforce, some with protection and others without. Those who decide not to opt out are protected against detriment and dismissal, since whether or not to opt out is an entirely free choice. The employer has a duty to take reasonable steps to ensure that the tier who has not opted out do not work longer than the 48-hour maximum on average, potentially increasing the burden during busier times on the tier which has opted out (subject to their rest entitlements (see Chapter 3)).

Employers, however, do need to identify those at risk of breaching the limit and put in place procedures to minimise the risk. One way is to write to all staff individually, explaining the obligations under the Regulations and asking them for their views on whether they should or would wish to opt out. This letter should also ask them to notify the employer of any additional external work or whether they wish to undertake voluntary overtime, which may have the effect of taking them over the limit. Whether or not to opt out must be a free choice for the worker; an employer cannot seek to require opt-outs in the normal course. Communications with workers should make this clear.

Where, however, a worker wishes to be granted voluntary overtime or wishes to take a second job in circumstances where the first employer's agreement is needed, the employer would be in a position to secure an opt-out as part of the "deal". This will inevitably be a fertile area for cases in the next couple of years, as the extent of the employer's obligation in these circumstances is clarified.

It is also worth remembering that opt-out agreements can last for specified periods only (for example to cover a particular project) and be terminable on as little as seven days' notice. In some circumstances, a more limited opt out agreement may be satisfactory to both parties, in circumstances where an ongoing one terminable by three months' notice may not be.

9.4 Examples

An example opt-out agreement is found in the Appendix.

10. Record Keeping

10.1 Under the Opt-Out Agreement

The employer must maintain up to date records which:

(a)   identify each worker who has opted out;

(b)   set out the terms of the opt-out agreement, for example how long the agreement is to last and the notice period; and

(c)   specify the number of hours worked by that individual for the employer during each reference period since the agreement came into effect.

These records must be kept for at least two years.

The employer must therefore be in a position to demonstrate the **actual** hours worked by each individual worker who has opted out. These records must be made available for inspection by the Health and Safety Executive or the local authority Environmental Health Officer, as appropriate, and at any time.

10.2 Record Keeping Generally

In respect of those workers who have not agreed to opt out, the employer nevertheless has a general duty under Regulation 9 to keep records –

(a) *"which are adequate to show whether the [48-hour limit is] being complied with in the case of each worker employed by him in relation to whom [it] applies; and*

(b) *retain such records for two years from the date on which they were made".*

10.3 Keeping Track of Hours

For some this will be straightforward: for workers who are paid by the hour, pay records will probably do the trick. For others, shift patterns or clock card records will demonstrate the hours spent in the workplace, requiring a simple deduction of any periods of time which are not classified as working time, for example lunch and other breaks.

The office/salaried staff environment gives rise to greater practical issues, particularly for those who have not been asked before to keep account of their hours. Again, those workers whose hours over and above the normal office hours are recorded, for example for overtime purposes, are unlikely to present a problem. It is workers who are required to work such additional hours as may be necessary for the proper performance of their duties, for no additional pay, who are the bigger issue. Each employer must devise a system, compatible with its working environment, which is able to keep track of individual working hours. The most obvious method is to ask each worker to keep a note of what time they arrive and what time they leave each day and whether or not they are required to work through lunch, and for the employer to monitor the system to make sure it continues effectively.

Monitoring is not only important to make sure that the hours are being recorded regularly, but also to identify any individuals who might be at risk of exceeding the limits, so that work can be reorganised or reallocated as appropriate, or an opt-out agreement sought.

11. What Are The Penalties?

11.1 Breach of Employers' Duty

An employer who fails to take all reasonable steps to ensure that the 48-hour maximum average is not exceeded commits a criminal offence, and is liable to a fine of up to £5,000 within the Magistrates Court and an unlimited fine in the Crown Court (see Chapter 7 – Enforcement and Remedies for further details, including prosecution policy and procedure).

11.2 Claims by Workers

Workers have the right not to work in excess of the average 48-hour limit, unless they opt out, on an individual basis. Where, in the absence of such an opt-out, a worker's working time exceeds this limit during the relevant reference period, the worker can refuse to continue working until his/her average working hours meet the requirement. This decision was taken by the High Court in the case of *Barber and others v R J B Mining UK Limited,* 3 March 1999. A worker exercising this right will require very careful managing. Penalising the worker – up to and including dismissal – in such circumstances would attract the enhanced employment protection rights provided for by the Regulations (see Chapter 7 – Enforcement and Remedies).

CHAPTER 3

Rest periods

1. **Introduction**

   1.1 Entitlements and Obligations

   Regulations 10, 11 and 12 provide workers with additional protection, by restricting the number of hours an individual can work without being entitled to:

   (a) a rest break;

   (b) daily rest at the end of the working day or night;

   (c) weekly rest – time off every week or fortnight.

   It should be noted that these periods are "entitlements". The Government has indicated within the DTI Guidance, which accompanied the Regulations, and also in the 1998 consultation document, that if workers choose not to exercise their entitlements then the employer would not be breaching the Regulations.

   1.2 Link with Health and Safety

   It is important to remember that the principal objective of the EC Directive is to safeguard the health and safety of workers and to protect them from over-work. Therefore, at the very least, it is important for employers to provide the opportunities and to encourage workers to exercise their entitlements to rest periods. Employers should also bear in mind the general duties under the Health & Safety At Work Act 1974 to take all steps reasonably practicable to ensure the health, safety and welfare at work of all employees. Those who disregard the rest entitlements and ambivalently allow workers to work through long periods of time, without taking adequate rest, are arguably failing to meet their obligations under the 1974 Act irrespective of the position under the Regulations.

1.3 Minimum Entitlements

The minimum rest breaks and rest periods required by the Regulations are set out below. However, employers can give greater rest breaks and rest periods in their contracts of employment should they so wish.

Before looking at the minimum entitlements in detail, it is necessary to understand the distinction between "rest periods" and "working time" and the Regulations have specific definitions for this purpose.

1.4 Young Workers

Young workers have entitlements to longer breaks than adult workers. This chapter focuses on adult workers. Where your workers are under the age of 18, please see Chapter 6 – Young Workers.

2. What is a Rest Period?

2.1 Basic Definitions

Under Regulation 2(1) a rest period is defined in relation to a worker as *"a period which is not working time, other than a rest break or leave to which the worker is entitled under these Regulations"*.

The definition of working time in relation to a worker at Regulation 2(1) is as follows:

"(a) any period during which [a worker] is working, at his employer's disposal and carrying out his activity or duties;

(b) any period during which [a worker] is receiving relevant training;

(c) any additional period which is to be treated as working time for the purpose of these Regulations under a relevant agreement;

and "work" shall be construed accordingly".

Bearing in mind the definitions of working time and rest periods under the Regulations, many employers would benefit from incorporating an agreed definition of time that will be considered to be working time and time that will be considered to be rest periods into a working time policy or within the body of a relevant agreement.

2.2 Which Activities Are Working Time?

As stated in Chapter 2, for time to be considered to be working time, all elements of the definition must be satisfied, therefore businesses will need to consider the position in respect of the following types of activity.

Employers should be looking to consider "standby" or "on call" as a rest period until such time as a worker is required to specifically carry out activities or duties. This might include, for example, a solicitor required to attend at a police station, or an engineer on call-out duty needed at the plant.

It has been reported in the December 1998 edition of the IDS Brief that a Spanish case is to challenge the EC Directive (No. 93/104) on the basis that on-call duty is not working time in the Spanish case of *Sindicato de Médicos de Asistencia Pública (Simap) v Conselleria de Sanidad y Consumo de la Generalidad Valenciana (C-303/98)*. Whilst this may be understandable in the sense that people who are "on call", and also people that are required to stay away at hotels for business purposes, are not able to pursue their own interests and activities and are at their employer's disposal, to consider this time as working time will clearly be inconsistent with the intention of the Directive and the Regulations.

This is because the ethos behind the Directive is to safeguard the health, safety and welfare of workers and to prevent them from being over-worked and working too many hours. There will be significant periods of time when such workers, although at their employer's disposal, are not carrying out their activities and duties and are free to take rest. In most cases, workers will be adequately compensated for being on call by receiving extra remuneration under their contracts of employment, However, once again, just because they are in receipt of payment for this time, for the purposes of these Regulations, it should still not be considered to be working time.

Other problematic areas which ought to be defined by a relevant agreement or a working time policy are as follows:

(a)   travelling to and from different sites;

(b)   home working where an employee has taken work home;

(c)   attending lunches/evening meals on business.

These areas are likely to be the subject of much negotiation between employers and employee representatives. As well as dealing with these difficult periods of time, all lunch breaks and tea breaks should be clearly defined as rest breaks, regardless of whether or not the individual receives payment.

2.3 The Benefits of Agreements

In summary, therefore, it would be prudent for larger businesses and companies to define in a working time policy or a relevant agreement not only working time but also those periods which can be considered to be either rest breaks or rest entitlements under the Regulations, as this will ensure that both the employer and the workers clearly understand the distinction between the different periods of time.

3. Daily Rest

Under Regulation 10 a worker is entitled to a rest period of not less than 11 consecutive hours in each 24-hour period during which he works for his employer.

In effect, this Regulation stipulates that no worker should be compelled to work a shift in excess of 13 hours. The Regulations do not compel workers to take advantage of rest entitlements, but employers must take necessary measures to enable workers to take rest entitlements, even if they then decide to forego their entitlements.

4. Weekly Rest

Under Regulation 11 a worker is entitled to an uninterrupted rest period of not less than 24 hours in each seven day period during which he works for his employer. Alternatively, the weekly reference period can be averaged over a reference period of 14 days – this will leave the employer with two options:

(a) two uninterrupted rest periods each of not less than 24 hours in a 14 day period; or

(b) one uninterrupted rest period of not less than 48 hours in each such 14 day period.

If either of these rest periods is provided to a worker then this will replace the obligation to provide 24 hours rest in each seven day period.

It should be noted however, that weekly rest is in addition to a worker's daily rest entitlement. For example, if a worker has finished a shift on the sixth day of the working week, having worked all of the preceding days, he will be entitled to his 11-hour consecutive daily rest, together with a further weekly rest entitlement, making a total rest break of 35 hours.

If it is possible for the employer to justify including all or part of the daily entitlement in the weekly rest period on the grounds of objective or technical reasons, or reasons concerning the organisation of work, then this will be permitted. However, what constitutes objective or technical reasons is unclear from the Regulations. It would clearly have to be more than purely economic reasons and might relate to problems with plant or machinery, or emergency problems justifying such action on the part of the employer.

5. Rest Breaks

Where a worker's daily working time is more than six hours in duration, Regulation 12 provides that the worker is entitled to a rest break. Unless a collective agreement or workforce agreement provides otherwise, the rest break must be an uninterrupted period of not less than 20 minutes, and the worker is entitled to spend it away from his workstation if he has one.

Collective agreements and workforce agreements can provide for rest breaks of a more or less generous nature or can exclude them altogether. It should be noted, however, that where employers seek to reduce or remove the worker's rest break entitlement in this way, they will be required to provide compensatory rest (see Part 11.3 below).

6. Regulation 8 – Pattern of Work

Regulation 8 provides a general obligation on employers to ensure that workers are given adequate rest breaks where the work that they are undertaking is either monotonous or the work rate has been determined due to a particular pattern of work. The Government's DTI Guidance at paragraph 6.1.3 identifies such work as work on a production line where the work is continuously carrying out the same single task.

There is no guidance in either the Regulations or the Government's DTI Guidance as to how regular breaks should be provided and whether or not they are in addition to the basic 20-minute rest break for working time of more than six hours. The very fact, however, that this type of work has been specifically highlighted within the Regulations and identified as a potential hazard to the health, safety and welfare of workers means that employers should think seriously about providing regular or frequent breaks in the work pattern in order to satisfy their health and safety obligations.

7. Payment for Rest Periods

There will no doubt be considerable debate regarding the length and frequency of rest periods, given the potential impact on pay. There is no obligation on an employer under the Regulations to pay the worker during any of the rest periods. These are merely periods of time during which a worker is entitled to rest, to meet the aims and objectives of the Regulations.

A practical difficulty, however, is that many employees enjoy high levels of overtime to increase their earnings. If one result of this is a reduction in the number of rest periods taken, then the workers' working time will inevitably increase – potentially giving rise to a breach of the average 48-hour maximum working week unless an individual opt-out is agreed. In turn, this will lead to stringent record-keeping requirements – to record the actual hours worked by each worker in each reference period, which will highlight those workers who have not taken their rest entitlements. In the event of an illness or accident, such records could ultimately be used as evidence in support of a prosecution of the employer and also in any employer's liability or employment tribunal claim.

It is extremely important, therefore, that overtime is monitored correctly and that workers are fully aware of and are encouraged to exercise their entitlements to rest breaks and rest periods.

8. Unmeasured Working Time

Workers who are regarded as having unmeasured working time, in accordance with Regulation 20, will not be entitled to either daily rest, weekly rest or rest breaks.

Regulation 20 defines workers with unmeasured working time as workers where, on account of the specific characteristics of the activity in which they are engaged, the duration of their working time is not measured or predetermined or can be determined by the workers themselves, as may be the case for:

(a)   managing executives or other persons with autonomous decision-taking powers;

(b) family workers; or

(c) workers officiating at religious ceremonies in churches and religious communities.

The main area of concern is how widely employers can interpret the derogation applicable to managing executives or persons with autonomous decision-taking powers. Very few workers will have absolute autonomy over their roles and even directors of companies are ultimately responsible to the board. The interpretation of Regulation 20 is likely to be the subject matter of employment tribunal claims, due to the ambiguous nature of the drafting. Employers seeking to draw a wider interpretation of Regulation 20 would be advised to concentrate on the wording of the definition, which enables reliance on this exclusion on the basis that workers determine their own working time and manage their own workloads. Employers can then seek to maintain that, providing these individuals adequately meet their responsibilities and are not subject to monitoring or any particular time schedule, then they ought to be excluded from rest entitlements due to Regulation 20. However, companies would be sensible to adopt a cautious approach to Regulation 20 and not seek to be overly ambitious in its application.

When considering the overall definition it would ultimately be sensible to only rely upon it for the most senior personnel within an organisation who would clearly fall within the definition. Organisations will then be in a position to review their policy as and when case law develops and more guidance is provided by the employment tribunal.

9. The Impact of Regulation 21 – Special Cases

Regulation 21 stipulates that entitlements to daily rest, weekly rest and rest breaks do not apply in relation to workers in a range of special circumstances. These include:

(a) activities where the worker's place of work and his place of residence are distant from one another or where the worker's different places of work are distant from one another. This could potentially cover sales representatives who travel between various locations and may also cover workers who are required to travel to a temporary location of work. The travel time to this location is likely to be "working time" as it is a necessity of their job that they travel to a specific location. It would, however, mean that the daily rest entitlement cannot be avoided if the total working time, including the travel, exceeds 13 hours;

(b) security and surveillance activities requiring a permanent presence in order to protect property and persons, for example, security guards, caretakers or security firms;

(c) activities involving the need for continuity of service or production, for example:

   (i) services relating to the reception, treatment and/or care provided by hospitals or similar establishments, residential institutions and prisons;

   (ii) dock or airport workers;

   (iii) press, radio and television, cinematographic production, postal and telecommunications services and civil protection services;

   (iv) gas, water and electricity production, transmission and distribution, household refuse collection and incineration;

   (v) industries in which work cannot be interrupted on technical grounds: the technical reason would again have to be more than purely economic reasons;

   (vi) research and development activities;

   (vii) agriculture.

(d) where there is a foreseeable surge of activity within the work place as may be the case in relation to agriculture, tourism and postal services;

(e) finally, where the worker's activities are affected by:

   (i) an occurrence due to unusual and unforeseeable circumstances beyond the control of the employer;

   (ii) exceptional events, the consequences of which could not have been avoided despite the exercise of all due care by the employer; or

   (iii) an accident or the imminent risk of an accident.

It can be seen from Regulation 21 that there is scope for an employer to vary or disapply rest entitlements for particular types of workers. If, however, an employer seeks to vary or disapply a worker's entitlement in reliance upon Regulation 21 then they will need to provide compensatory rest in accordance with Regulation 24 (see Part 11.3 below).

10. Shift Workers

Regulation 22 provides a specific derogation from daily rest and weekly rest for shift workers who, as a result of changing shifts, cannot take either a daily rest or weekly rest period between the end of one shift and the start of the next one.

It also specifically excludes workers from daily and weekly rest entitlements where they are engaged in activities involving periods of work split up over the day, for example, cleaning staff.

A shift worker is defined as a worker whose work schedule is part of shift work, and shift work is defined as any method of organising work in shifts whereby workers succeed each other at the same workstations according to a certain pattern, including a rotating pattern, and which may be either continuous or discontinuous but entails the need for workers to work at different times over a given period of days or weeks.

This derogation will prevent employers from having to rearrange and alter shift patterns where they organise work in accordance with continental shift patterns, for example mornings, afternoons and nights. Often workers are required to "double-back" and commence night shifts, for example, after just finishing a session of morning shifts.

Once again this derogation is subject to providing alternative compensatory rest to such workers who would otherwise be entitled to daily or weekly rests. However, it would normally be the case that workers engaged in such shift patterns would receive at least an equivalent period of compensatory rest within a reasonable period of time by merely properly performing their work in accordance with the shift pattern which would ordinarily provide breaks in working time and significant rest periods.

11. How can Rest Entitlements be Varied?

11.1 Collective and Workforce Agreements

If an employer relies upon Regulation 21 – (special cases) and Regulation 22 (shift workers) to be able to vary rest entitlements, then there will be no requirement to enter into a collective or workforce agreement to obtain this derogation. If the employer is satisfied that Regulation 21 or 22 applies to a particular worker then there is no necessity to collectively bargain with the workforce to introduce a general right to vary rest entitlements. It is, however, possible to introduce within a collective or workforce agreement (providing such an agreement has been properly constituted and meets all required obligations) a right to generally vary rest entitlements.

However, such an agreement is only likely to be reached if the workforce or the union can be satisfied that compensatory rest has been properly provided for within such an agreement.

11.2 Individual Opt-Out Agreements

Unlike the maximum weekly working time as stipulated by Regulation 4, it is not possible for individuals to reach an agreement with their employer to generally waive their rights to rest entitlements under Regulations 10, 11 and 12. Employers who have obtained an opt-out in respect of the maximum weekly working time should not, therefore, take the view that there are no longer any restrictions on the amount of time that the worker can work for them. All employees and workers, regardless of whether they have signed an individual opt-out, should still be given the opportunity to exercise their rest entitlements. It will therefore be important for employers to continue to monitor working hours and, wherever possible, ensure that workers are not working excessive overtime which encroaches into their rest periods.

11.3 Compensatory Rest

Compensatory rest under Regulation 24 is an equivalent period of rest to which a worker will be entitled in lieu of either rest breaks, daily rest or weekly rest in circumstances where such rest periods have not been provided, by virtue of Regulations 21 or 22 or due to modifications under a collective or workforce agreement.

The Government's DTI guidance states that it should ordinarily be possible to provide an equivalent period of compensatory rest within a couple of weeks for daily rest and within a couple of months for weekly rest.

With regards to rest breaks, the Government's DTI guidance makes it clear that where rest breaks are modified it will not be possible for the rest break to be added to the beginning or the end of a worker's shift as there should be a break in the working time.

In exceptional cases where it is not possible, for objective reasons, to grant such a period of rest, the employer must afford the worker such protection as may be appropriate in order to safeguard the worker's health and safety (Regulation 24(6)).

Once again, the Regulations do not consider what steps employers should take to meet this obligation. If a worker is clearly not being given the opportunity to exercise rest entitlements on a consistent basis and, for example, suffers an accident, it would be extremely difficult for an employer to demonstrate that they have taken all steps reasonably practicable to discharge their obligations properly in protecting the worker's health and safety. Therefore it would be unwise for an employer not to provide compensatory rest if choosing to disapply daily or weekly rest in the hope that they can rely upon Regulation 24(b).

CHAPTER 4

Night workers

1. Introduction

Over the last ten years employers have been under pressure to ensure that capital expenditure is used more effectively, resulting in an increase in the number of employees working shifts.

Night working, traditional fixed night shifts and modern rotating shift patterns have the potential to vastly increase efficient use of equipment and premises.

However, since October 1998 the Working Time Regulations now impose significant limits on the amount and types of work which can be done at night.

In broad terms, employers are required to take all reasonable steps to ensure that night workers do not work more than an average of eight hours in 24 over a 17-week averaging period.

2. What is the Night?

The Regulations provide a definition of night time which will apply in default of any other choice made in a relevant agreement. The default provision defines night time as the period of seven hours between 11:00pm and 6:00am. A relevant agreement (see Chapter 2) may stipulate that night time be some other period which lasts for seven hours and includes the hours between 12:00pm and 5:00am, e.g. 10:00pm to 5:00am or 12:00pm to 7:00am.

The nature and specific provisions relating to relevant agreements are discussed in Chapter 2, Part 5.6, but in broad terms a relevant agreement includes a workforce agreement made with elected employee representatives, any provision of a collective agreement with a recognised trade union, or any other agreement in writing which is legally enforceable, such as a contract of employment.

This means that the employer can effectively use the contract of employment to minimise the number of hours an individual works during the night time, thus reducing the average night hours worked. The night working limits apply only to night workers, that is those who work at least three hours during night time and, where night time can be restricted, the number of workers qualifying as night workers may be reduced.

Further detailed explanations of the definition of a night worker are set out below but, as an example, pub workers may be required to work after 11:00pm but may finish before 2:00am. If in these circumstances the default definition of night time is applied, then such individuals will be working three hours during the night and, in the absence of other factors which exclude them, are likely to be night workers. If the employer were to specify in the contract that the night time begins only at midnight and lasts until 7:00am, only employees regularly working after 3:00am in the morning will be night workers. Clearly the same principles apply to early risers where the start of the seven-hour period can be brought forward to 10:00am so that the night ends at 5:00am. Only individuals working regularly before 2:00am will then be night workers and the less restrictive average working week provisions will apply (see Chapter 2).

3. Night Workers

On the face of it the definition of a night worker is quite straightforward. The Regulations provide that *"a night worker means a worker –*

(a) *who, as a normal course, works at least three hours of his daily working time during night time; or*

(b) *who is likely, during night time, to work at least such proportion of his annual working time as may be specified for the purposes of these Regulations in a collective agreement or a workforce agreement;*

and, for the purpose of paragraph (a) of this definition, a person works hours as a normal course (without prejudice to the generality of that expression) if he works such hours on the majority of days on which he works".

A strict interpretation of this provision suggests that it excludes those workers who do not work at least three hours during the night on the majority of days worked. This means that, for example, workers undertaking rotating 12-hour shift patterns may not be covered since they only work during night hours on 50% of the days they work. Again, individuals undertaking rotating continental shift patterns may not be night workers since they will, depending on how the night time is defined, be unlikely to work during it on more than one-third of the days on which they work. This interpretation is supported by the terms of the European Directive which defines a night worker as one who works at night on a majority of days. Note, the Regulations must be interpreted consistently with the Directive (see Chapter 1).

This interpretation of the provision is, however, undermined by the inclusion in the Regulations' definition of the words *"without prejudice to the generality of that expression"*. The DTI Guidance (see Chapter 1) suggests that where individuals work shifts which include night hours on a regular basis, whether or not these shifts form the majority of their working hours, they will still be night workers.

If this interpretation is correct then individuals working, only one night shift per month, provided this is on a regular and defined basis, may be night workers for the purposes of the Regulations. Indeed there is no reason, then, why those who work at night time during peak demand periods during the year, where these occur on a regular basis, might not also be night workers. This was the view taken by the High Court in Northern Ireland in the case of *R V Attorney General for Northern Ireland ex parte Burns* (IDS Brief 635 p.9). The High Court decided that a person working at night on one week in three was a "night worker" for the purposes of the Directive. It seems likely that the Regulations will be given a similar interpretation.

4. The Limit – Normal Working Hours

The limit on the number of hours a night worker can work is based on the normal working hours the individual undertakes. Unlike the 48-hour limit, normal working hours do not necessarily correspond with actual hours worked.

The definition of normal working hours is set out in section 234 of the Employment Rights Act 1996:

"(1) Where an employee is entitled to overtime pay when employed for more than a fixed number of hours in a week or other period, there are for the purposes of this Act normal working hours in his case.

(2) Subject to subsection (3), the normal working hours in such a case are the fixed number of hours.

(3) Where in such a case –

> (a) the contract of employment fixes the number, or minimum number, of hours of employment in a week or other period (whether or not it also provides for the reduction of that number or minimum in certain circumstances), and
>
> (b) that number or minimum number of hours exceeds the number of hours without overtime,
>
> the normal working hours are that number or minimum number of hours (and not the number of hours without overtime)."

4.1 Overtime

This definition means that where employees are required to undertake a minimum amount of contractual overtime that overtime should be included in the calculation of normal working hours for the purposes of the night working limit. Where the employee is not contractually bound to undertake a fixed minimum amount of overtime, or where any overtime undertaken is voluntary, such hours do not count toward normal working time for the purposes of the limit.

This means that night workers may work voluntary overtime bringing them well above the notional limits on night working and, provided the individual opt-out is completed, then the average 48-hour working week restrictions will also be complied with. Voluntary overtime can therefore be used by organisations to overcome some of the restrictions placed on night working provided, of course, such overtime is made sufficiently attractive to individual employees. It provides flexibility in circumstances where employers are unable to reach workforce agreements with recognised trade unions or elected representatives (discussed below) to disapply the Regulations. However, employers should, when seeking to rely on these provisions, note the requirements of Regulation 10 which specifies that all employees are entitled to a minimum daily rest period of not less than 11 hours in each consecutive 24 hour period. This rest break provision has previously been discussed in Chapter 3.

4.2 Daily Rest Breaks

Normal working hours will include periods of rest at work whether under the Working Time Regulations or under specific contractual provisions.

The Working Time Directive (Directive 93/104/EC) states that "research has shown that the human body is more sensitive at night to environmental disturbances and also to certain burdens and forms of work organisation and that long periods of night work can be detrimental to the health of workers and can endanger safety at the workplace.

There is a need to limit the duration of periods of night work, including overtime, and to provide for employers who regularly use night workers to bring this information to the attention of the competent authorities if they so request."

The purpose of the Working Time Directive is to minimise the length of time spent at work (rather than working) during the night because of the disruption this causes to health and sleep patterns. UK courts are obliged to interpret the Regulations consistently with the purpose of the Directive (see Chapter 1). This requires the calculation of normal working hours to include hours at work but not working.

4.3 Annual Hours

Where employees work annual hours it is unclear how normal working hours should be calculated since the Regulations clearly envisage a calculation for the purposes of the 17-week averaging period, based on contractual hours rather than hours actually worked.

If an annual hours contract specifies that a certain minimum or maximum number of hours will be worked in any week (e.g. a banked hours scheme) then the calculation of normal working hours will be based on those contractual hours. Where, however, no minimum and no maximum contractual hours are set, then it remains to be seen how the average will be calculated. Logically, and based on the assumption that it is average shift length which is being assessed, the annual hours should be divided by the number of weeks in the year, thus producing normal working hours.

$$\text{i.e.:} \quad \frac{\text{Annual hours}}{52} = \text{Normal Working Hours}$$

However, instances of such truly flexible working practices are rare. In most circumstances those with an annual hours contract will have identifiable shift patterns and an identifiable number of hours they can be asked to work in any one-week period. This will then form the normal working hours.

5. Reference Period

The basic reference period applying to night working is 17 weeks. In the absence of a relevant agreement this 17-week period can be any 17 weeks during the individual's employment. It is a rolling referencing period.

Like the 48-hour limit, this referencing period can, by concluding a relevant agreement, be made successive, i.e. the averaging occurs for each referencing period. This has the advantage both of providing certainty in that it facilitates record keeping and calculation, but also of allowing employees to undertake short bursts of longer working during periods of peak demand which can then be averaged over the other weeks in each successive averaging period. For example the eight-hour maximum can be exceeded during the last weeks of one referencing period and at the start of the next, provided the average is not exceeded in each referencing period.

If an organisation has a peak of demand during July and August of each year, then the contract of employment may provide that night workers must undertake compulsory overtime subject to certain minima during this period. Compulsory overtime will be normal working hours and will be included in the calculation of average night work. If averaging periods are made successive and July forms part of the end of one averaging period, with August at the start of another, then the extra hours being worked during those two months can be "clawed back" for the purposes of the Regulations by ensuring there is a reduction in hours at the start of the first referencing period and later on during the remainder of the second referencing period.

5.1 New Workers

New employees joining an organisation have their first referencing period based on the number of weeks worked. For example, if they have only worked for two weeks, during those weeks the new night worker may not work an average of more than eight hours in any 24 based on a two week averaging period, i.e. he/she will not have been entitled to work longer than 96 hours in two weeks.

5.2 Calculating the Average

Regulation 6(5) sets out how the averaging process works:

"A night worker's average normal hours of work for each 24 hours during a reference period shall be determined according to the formula –

$$\frac{A}{B - C}$$

where –

A is the number of hours during the reference period which are normal working hours for that worker;

B is the number of days during the reference period; and

C is the total number of hours during the reference period comprised in rest periods spent by the worker in pursuance of his entitlement under regulation 11, divided by 24."

Assuming that the reference period of 17 weeks is not altered (as discussed below) and that the employer has determined that the weekly rest periods (discussed in Chapter 3) will be taken as a weekly period of 24 hours the calculation will be:

$$\frac{\text{contractual hours (including contractual minimum overtime)}}{119 - 17}$$

Clearly the calculation will be altered where either:

(a) the reference period is changed by collective agreement (as discussed below); or

(b) the employer has specified that the weekly rest break is taken in 48-hour blocks over a 14-day period, and this means that in the given reference period fewer hours are spent on rest breaks.

6. Exclusions

Regulation 20 provides that the night working maximum does not apply to a worker where *"on account of the specific characteristics of the activity in which he is engaged, the duration of his working time is not measured or predetermined or can be determined by the worker himself."*

Examples given are:

(a) managing executives or other persons with autonomous decision-taking powers; and

(b) family workers; or

(c) workers officiating at religious ceremonies in churches and religious communities.

A further detailed discussion of the kind of workers who fit into this category is in Chapter 2 but it should be noted that the obligations in respect of health assessments, recording of hours, transfer to day work and monotonous work will still apply to these workers.

6.1 Special Cases

Regulation 21 provides that the night working limit does not apply in relation to a worker:

(a) *"Where the worker's activities are such that his place of work and place of residence are distant from one another or his different places of work are distant from one another."*

The DTI Guidance indicates that the sort of situation which is envisaged is where *"because of the distance from home, it is desirable for them to work longer hours for a short period to complete the task more quickly or where continual changes in the location of work make it impractical to set a pattern of work"*.

Although it is tempting to view this provision as excluding from the night working limits all those who undertake business travel on a regular basis, the flexibility this derogation appears to offer is limited by two factors:

(i) the requirement to interpret the Regulations purposively so that any limitations on the rules which are intended to protect workers' health and safety are strictly interpreted; and

(ii) because workers are entitled to compensatory rest where the provisions relating to night working are disapplied (see below).

(b) Workers whose *"activities involve the need for continuity of service or production as, may be the case in relation to –*

   (i) *services relating to the reception, treatment or care provided by hospitals or similar establishments, residential institutions and prisons;*

   (ii) *work at docks or airports;*

   (iii) *press, radio, television, cinematographic production, postal and telecommunications services and civil protection services;*

   (iv) *gas, water and electricity production, transmission and distribution, household refuse collection and incineration;*

   (v) *industries in which work cannot be interrupted on technical grounds;*

   (vi) *research and development activities;*

   (vii) *agriculture"*.

Again these provisions are likely to be interpreted narrowly so that the need for continuity of service or production will have to be an almost absolute requirement rather than a desirable and efficiency-enhancing device before workers are excluded.

(c) Areas *"where there is a foreseeable surge of activity as may be the case in relation to –*

   (i) *agriculture;*

   (ii) *tourism; and*

   (iii) *postal services"*.

These provisions are likely to be interpreted to deal only with short surges of activity. It will therefore not be possible to rely upon this exclusion where the surge lasts for more than a few weeks or months.

(d) Finally, the regulations contain "Act of God" provisions common in European legal systems which allow the Regulations to be disapplied where *"the worker's activities are affected by –*

  (i) *an occurrence due to unusual and unforeseeable circumstances, beyond the control of the worker's employer;*

  (ii) *exceptional events, the consequences of which could not have been avoided despite the exercise of all due care by the employer; or*

  (iii) *an accident or the imminent risk of an accident".*

6.2 Domestic Service

Those who work as domestic servants do not have the protection of the night working limits nor are they subject to the provisions relating to health assessments, transfer to day work or monotonous work patterns. Records of hours worked will still need to be kept as set out below.

6.3 Work Involving Special Hazards or Heavy Physical or Mental Strain

Where work involves heavy physical or mental strain or other special hazards the referencing period is wholly disapplied. This means that these night workers cannot work any longer than eight hours in any 24-hour period.

Work involves special hazards or heavy physical or mental strain if:

"(a) it is identified as such in –

  (i) *a collective agreement, or*

  (ii) *a workforce agreement*

  which takes account of the specific effects and hazards of night work, or

(b) it is recognised in a risk assessment made by the employer under Regulation 3 of the Management of Health and Safety at Work Regulations 1992(a) as involving a significant risk to the health or safety of workers employed by him."

(Regulation 6(8))

It is worth noting that these are either/or provisions and it is not possible to agree in a collective or workforce agreement that a risk identified under an appropriate risk assessment does not involve special hazards.

6.4 Monotonous Work

The Regulations identify monotonous work patterns as involving special risks to the health and safety of workers. Regulation 8 indicates that:

"Where the pattern according to which an employer organises work is such as to put the health and safety of a worker employed by him at risk, in particular because the work is monotonous or the work-rate is predetermined, the employer shall ensure that the worker is given adequate rest breaks".

Arguably, if the risks associated with monotonous work are worthy of a particular Regulation then they are likely to amount to special hazard's for the purposes of the night working limits.

7. Flexibilities – Collective and Workforce Agreements

Collective and workforce agreements can modify or exclude the application of the maximum night working limit and the maximum limit in relation to work involving special hazards.

For more details regarding collective and workforce agreements, see Chapter 1.

8. Compensatory Rest – Where Exclusions Apply

Where the limits on night working or limits in respect of work involving special hazards are excluded, either under the special circumstances rules (above) or by a collective or workforce agreement, then the employer is required under Regulation 24 to provide:

"(a) ...an equivalent period of compensatory rest, and

(b) in exceptional cases in which it is not possible, for objective reasons, to grant such a period of rest, his employer shall afford him such protections as may be appropriate in order to safeguard the worker's health and safety".

It is difficult to see how these provisions will work in practice in relation to those employees who agree, on a collective basis, to exclude the average maximum in relation to night working. In practice those employees who agree to work in excess of the limit are likely not to be in a position to take compensatory rest for each period worked in excess of the eight-hour limit. In the context of night working, therefore, it is much more likely that the Regulations will require employers to carry out regular risk assessments and to provide other protection, where this is available, to safeguard employees' health and safety, e.g. canteen facilities, regular rest breaks, etc.

9. Some Common Shift Patterns Considered

9.1 Rotating Continental Eight Hour Shift Patterns (10:00 – 18:00, 18:00 – 02:00, 02:00 – 10:00 Monday – Friday)

If the restrictive interpretation of the definition of night workers advocated by the DTI guidance is accepted, then all individuals working this shift pattern who rotate will be night workers for the purposes of the Regulations.

Since the shift pattern is based on the eight-hour model, where there is no provision for compulsory overtime in the contract, the pattern will not breach the night working limits whether the work involves special hazards or not.

Where the work does not involve special hazards, weekly rest is given in 24-hour blocks and the 17-week referencing period applies then:

A = 680

B = 119

C = 17

$$\frac{680}{119 - 17} = 6.6$$

so that each worker is undertaking an average of 6.6 hours in 24 over the referencing period.

This means that compulsory overtime of one shift per week, or 136 hours per 17-week referencing period, can be required. Voluntary overtime is unlimited (subject to the maximum working week and individual opt-outs).

9.2 12-Hour Rotating, four on, four off (06:00 – 18:00, 18:00 – 06:00 Monday – Sunday)

Based on the DTI Guidance all regularly rotating workers will be night workers for the purpose of the regulations. The maximum number of shifts an individual could work over a 17-week referencing period, based on this shift pattern, is 60 shifts of 12 hours:

A = 720

B = 119

$$\frac{720}{119 - 17} = 7.05$$

C = 17

so that each worker works an average of 7.05 hours in 24 over the referencing period.

This means that the shift pattern complies with the night working averaging requirements and a maximum of eight 12-hour shifts can be required as compulsory overtime during each 17-week referencing period. Again, unlimited voluntary overtime can be worked.

9.3 Eight-Hour Shifts (Monday – Friday) and Two 12-Hour Shifts on One in Three Weekends

Weekend working is 24 hours on a maximum of six weekends within any referencing period.

Therefore:

A = 824

B = 119

$$\frac{824}{119 - 17} = 8.08 \text{ (approx)}$$

C = 17

Based on this pattern night workers are working an average of 8.08 (approximately) hours in 24 over each 17-week referencing period and will therefore exceed the limit on average night work hours.

Options:

(a) to argue that those workers operating rotating shifts do not fall within the definition of night workers as discussed above;

(b) alter or exclude the night working limit by means of a collective or workforce agreement; or

(c) undertake a contract change to reduce compulsory hours worked.

10. Keeping Records

Employers are required to keep adequate records to show that the limits on night work are being complied with and that health assessments (see below) have been done. Record keeping is further examined in Chapters 2 and 7. Records in respect of night working must be kept for two years.

11. Health Assessment

The Regulations require employers to provide night workers with the opportunity of:

(a) a health assessment before the employee begins night work; and

(b) health assessments carried out on a regular basis thereafter. It is worth noting that these health assessments must be subject to medical confidentiality.

Health assessments must be offered to employees and can be undertaken either by means of an appropriate questionnaire prepared by an appropriate healthcare professional and then interpreted by such an individual, or by medial examination. They should be offered before the worker begins night work and at least annually thereafter although no specific time-frame for repeat assessments is set out in the regulations. For existing employees currently working during the night, the DTI Guidance recommends that health assessments be offered as soon as possible.

It is worth noting that the health assessments, whether they are carried out by a medical practitioner or not, cannot be disclosed to any person other than the employee about whom they are made unless: he or she gives their consent; the disclosure is simply a statement that the individual is fit to undertake night work, or a health assessment has previously been undertaken for an earlier assignment and there is no reason to believe the prior assessment is no longer valid.

The DTI Guidance identifies a number of medical conditions which might increase the risks to individuals working at night in the workplace. In particular, the Guidance identifies the following as conditions which may be made worse by night work:

(1) *"Diabetes, particularly where treatment with insulin injections on a strict timetable is required.*

(2) *Some heart and circulatory disorders, particularly where factors such as physical stamina are affected.*

(3) *Stomach or intestinal disorders, such as ulcers and conditions where the timing of a meal is particularly important.*

(4) *Medical conditions affecting sleep.*

(5) *Some chronic chest disorders where night-time symptoms may be particularly troublesome.*

(6) *Other medical conditions requiring regular medication on a strict timetable."*

It is vital that practitioners conducting the health assessments, whether by questionnaire or by examination, should tailor their examination or questions and base these on the work that the individual carries out. It is therefore also vital that the health professional be fully informed as to the nature of the assessed employee's duties. The DTI Guidance indicates that, in some cases, asking employees to consult their own GPs for an assessment of whether they are fit for night work will be sufficient. However, employers will have to ensure that GPs are properly informed as to the nature of the work to be undertaken.

12. Transfer to Day Work

Where a health assessment identifies a health problem related to night work, or a medical practitioner certifies that an individual is suffering from a health problem which is connected with the fact that the worker performs night work, then the employer is under an obligation to consider whether that worker can be transferred to suitable work undertaken during the day. The obligation to transfer to day work is not absolute. Where, for example, the employer identifies that no day work is available then no transfer is necessary. In such situations, however, employers should also consider the provisions of the Disability Discrimination Act 1995 (DDA) which imposes special obligations to make reasonable adjustments to working conditions or arrangements where disabled persons are placed at a disadvantage.

13. Disabled Workers

The DDA 1995 defines a disabled person as someone with a physical or mental impairment which has a substantial or long-term effect on the ability of the individual to carry out normal day to day activities.

Normal day to day activities are defined as:

(a) mobility;

(b) manual dexterity;

(c) physical co-ordination;

(d) continence;

(e) ability to lift, carry or otherwise move everyday objects;

(f) speech, hearing or eyesight;

(g) memory, ability to concentrate, learn or understand;

(h) perception of the risk of physical danger.

"Long-term effect" can be shown where the impairment has lasted or is expected to last for 12 months or more, or lasts for life. In certain circumstances recurrent conditions will also be disabilities. Where an individual satisfies the definition then the employer is under a duty, where working arrangements or physical features of premises occupied by the employer place the disabled person at a substantial disadvantage in comparison to a person who is not disabled, to take such steps as are reasonably practicable to prevent the arrangements or features having that effect.

The DDA provides a number of examples of adjustments which include:

(1) transferring an individual to fill an existing vacancy;

(2) altering working hours;

(3) allowing the individual to be absent during working hours for rehabilitation, assessment or treatment.

These provisions mean that an employer, when faced with an individual with a disability which results in night working placing him or her at a substantial disadvantage, will be required to consider adjusting that working condition and whether a transfer to day work is possible. Notwithstanding the obligation to transfer night workers where other work is available, employers should also consider providing more regular rest breaks, shortening night working shift patterns, providing facilities for short rests, etc.

The reasonableness of the adjustment is assessed according to:

(i) the extent to which taking steps would prevent the effect in question;

(ii) the extent to which it is practicable for the employer to take the step;

(iii) financial and other costs which would be incurred by the employer in taking the steps and the extent to which taking it would disrupt any of his activities;

(iv) the extent of the employer's financial and other resources;

(v) the availability to the employer of financial or other assistance with respect to taking steps.

Where the employer is under a duty to make a reasonable adjustment and fails to do so then this can be justified only if the reason for the failure is both material to the circumstances of the particular case and substantial. Where the obligation arises and is not complied with – if the employer subsequently treats the disabled person less favourably on grounds of their disability (i.e. by dismissing them or reducing their pay) than they would treat others who were not disabled – then such less favourable treatment cannot be justified. The only exception would be if, having made all reasonable adjustments, it would still have been justifiable to penalise the employee.

14. Pregnant Workers

Special provisions also apply to pregnant workers.

The Management of Health and Safety at Work Regulations 1992 require employers to assess risks to which pregnant workers, those who are breastfeeding and new mothers are exposed. If a risk assessment reveals a risk to such an individual then the employer is under an obligation to take whatever preventative or protective measures are required by the specific legislation which covers the hazard concerned or, if none, to take reasonable steps to control the risk – which may include adjusting the employee's hours of work or working conditions.

This means that the employer, faced with a pregnant worker who may be suffering from night work-related health issues, should again consider not just transferring the individual to day work but perhaps reducing working hours so that the risk is avoided. Where this is not possible then the employer is under an obligation to provide the individual with suitable alternative work which is both appropriate and on not substantially less favourable terms than those under which the affected employee normally works.

Factors which are relevant as to whether or not the work is suitable include:

(a)   status;

(b)   the nature of the work;

(c)   place of work;

(d)   travelling time;

(e)   pay;

(f)   hours;

(g)   working conditions generally.

Where no suitable alternative employment is available then the employer is under an obligation to suspend the employee on full pay. Only where the employee unreasonably refuses to perform suitable alternative work does the right to remuneration cease.

CHAPTER 5

Holiday entitlement

1. The Entitlement

Regulation 13 of the Working Time Regulations (the Regulations) provides that a worker is entitled in each leave year to three weeks' paid leave, rising to four weeks' after the 23rd November 1999.

In any leave year commencing after the 23rd November 1998, but before the 23rd November 1999, a worker is entitled to three weeks' paid annual leave, together with a proportion of the fourth week which is calculated by ascertaining the number of days that overlap between the 23rd November 1998 and the commencement of the new annual leave year.

The following example is contained within the DTI's Guidance to the Regulations: if a worker's leave year starts on the 1st January and they work five days a week, then their entitlement for 1999 is three weeks (15 days) plus a proportion of a further week.

The additional part week is calculated by multiplying the number of working days in the workers' normal working week by the number of days between the 23rd November and the start of the leave year, divided by the number of days in a year.

In this case, there are 39 days between the 23rd November and the start of the leave year, so the calculation is:

$$\frac{5 \text{ days} \times 39}{365} = 0.53$$

This is rounded up to the nearest day i.e. one day. This means that the worker is entitled to 16 days paid annual leave for the leave year 1999.

2. Qualifying Period

The entitlement conferred by Regulation 13 does not arise until a worker has been continuously employed for 13 weeks. In order to be deemed to have been continuously employed for 13 weeks, the workers' relationship with the employer will have to have been governed by a contract (verbal or written) during the whole or part of each of those weeks.

Albeit this is not specified by the Regulations, the DTI Guidance, together with their further supplement *A Guide to Working Time Regulations,* seem to suggest that once workers have obtained the necessary qualifying period, i.e. 13 weeks continuous employment for the employer, they will then be subject to the full leave entitlement. Their full period of employment, including the 13 weeks' qualifying period, will be taken into account when calculating that entitlement.

3. When Does the Leave Year Commence?

A worker's leave year under the Regulations begins on any date during the calendar year as provided for in a relevant agreement or, where there are no applicable provisions, the leave year will begin on the 1st October 1998 for workers whose employment began before that date. Alternatively, if the worker's employment begins after the 1st October 1998, the leave year begins on the date on which the employment begins and each subsequent anniversary of that date.

In accordance with Regulation 13(5), where the start of the leave year is specified in a relevant agreement and the worker's employment begins in the middle of the leave year, the annual leave entitlement will be reduced to ensure that it is proportionate to the amount of the leave year actually worked. For example, if he works six months of the leave year, he will be entitled to six months' annual leave entitlement, namely 1½ weeks. In this situation, as in the case of calculating a proportion of the fourth week for annual leave years commencing between the 23rd November 1998 and 23rd November 1999, any fraction of a day will be treated as a whole day.

4. When May Leave be Taken?

Under Regulation 13(9), annual leave may only be taken in the leave year in which it is due and there is no statutory right to carry forward annual leave entitlement to the following leave year. However, there are many organisations which do allow for a proportion of the annual leave entitlement to be carried forward to the following year. This will still be permissible, provided that the worker is always permitted to exercise their minimum statutory paid annual leave entitlement.

Existing contracts of employment may also pose problems in light of the new Regulations. For example, where employees accrue paid holiday leave during their first year of employment but are not entitled to exercise that leave until the following year – and thereafter accrued holiday in the second year will be taken in the third year and so on – this scheme is clearly non-compliant with the new Regulations for the first 12 months of the worker's employment. As a result, where employees have less than 12 months' service and are working under a contract of this nature, modification will have to be made between the parties to ensure that at least the minimum statutory requirement is provided for in the first 12 months.

There could also be a potential problem with annualised hours contracts. Many such contracts do not provide for specific annual leave entitlement as these are built into the rest period for workers when they are not rostered to carry out their shifts. It may be that the annualised hours contract specifically refers to a certain number of days within the rest entitlement as annual leave. Where this is the case there is unlikely to be any problem. However, if annual leave is not specifically referred to within contracts of employment or annualised hours contracts and it is merely implied that the rest periods include any entitlement to annual leave, there is a potential for ambiguity which ought to be clarified.

The Regulations specifically state that annual leave may not be replaced by a payment in lieu unless the employment is terminated. This is to prevent employers offering financial inducements to employees not to take their annual leave and to ensure that workers who would otherwise accept a payment in lieu are not given that option, but instead exercise their right to their annual leave entitlement.

5. Payment in Lieu upon Termination

In accordance with Regulation 14 – where a worker's employment is terminated during the course of the leave year and, on the date of the termination, the worker has not exercised his full annual leave entitlement – the worker will be entitled to payment in lieu for untaken annual leave. The outstanding annual leave should be calculated from the proportion of the leave year which has already expired on a pro rata basis.

The sum due in each case may be set out in a relevant agreement. Alternatively, the Government leaflet "A Guide to Working Time Regulations" provides the following formula:

$$(\mathbf{A} \times \mathbf{B}) - \mathbf{C}$$

where:

A is the period of leave to which the worker is entitled to;

B is the proportion of the worker's leave year which expired before the employment ended;

C is the period of leave taken by the worker between the start of the leave year and the effective date of termination.

For example, in the case of a worker who works five days a week (i.e. 3 x 5 days, leave during the leave year) whose employment terminated six months into the leave year (i.e. half the leave year has expired) and has taken only three days. The calculation would be:

$$(15 \times 0.5) - 3 = 4.5$$

Therefore the employer should pay the worker the equivalent of 4½ days pay.

The Regulations allow for an employer to be compensated where the proportion of leave taken by the worker exceeds the proportion of the leave year that has expired upon termination. This can be either by payment or by undertaking additional work. The employer should seek to implement within contracts of employment a contractual clause which allows them to claw back such overpayments from any payments made to the worker.

6. Payment for Periods of Annual Leave

The Employment Rights Act 1996, sections 221 to 224, determines the amount of a week's pay. A normal week's pay is therefore:

(a) in the case of a worker with regular working hours what they would earn for a normal working week;

(b) in the case of a worker whose normal working hours vary from week to week, the average hourly rate of pay they normally get, multiplied by an average of their normal weekly working hours over the previous 12 weeks;

(c) in the case of a worker with no normal working hours, it is the average pay received over the previous 12 weeks.

Normal working hours are said to be the normal hours fixed by a contract of employment. Therefore overtime is not included within normal working hours unless there is a minimum number of stipulated overtime hours fixed by the contract over and above notional fixed hours.

Bearing in mind the above and the need to comply with Regulation 16, holiday credit schemes which allow workers to obtain their holiday entitlement by purchasing weekly credits to be exchanged for holidays at a later date may mean that the actual rate of pay for a holiday week does not correlate with what should in fact be paid.

It is also worthy of note that a worker's entitlement to receive payment during the statutory period of annual leave is not affected by a right to holiday pay under a contract of employment. Therefore a contract of employment may provide for more generous periods of paid annual leave than the statutory minimum and in such a case the contract would prevail. However, any payment made under the contract of employment for paid annual leave will go towards discharging the employer's liability to make payments under Regulation 16.

7. Dates On Which Leave May Be Taken

Regulation 15 sets out details of the stipulated procedures for workers requesting and giving notice of their intention to take annual leave and how this should be either confirmed or rejected by the employer.

It is possible to avoid the provisions contained within Regulation 15 by the employer and worker agreeing the procedure for requesting and granting annual leave within the body of a relevant agreement. Therefore, if an employer already stipulates the procedure for taking annual leave within either a contract of employment, a collective agreement or an accepted policy, then this will override Regulation 15. However, in the absence of such an agreement, it would be unwise for an employer to ignore the impact of Regulation 15. Ideally, a procedure for taking annual leave should be detailed in a relevant agreement whether it is the case that employees already receive a contractual entitlement over and above the statutory minimum or they are obtaining a paid annual leave entitlement for the first time under the Regulations.

In the absence of an agreed procedure, Regulation 15 provides that:

(a) it is possible for an employer to compel a worker to take all or part of their annual leave entitlement on particular days or part days providing the worker is given prior notice of at least twice as many days as leave to be taken;

(b) if a worker requires annual leave, they must give an employer details of the days or part days annual leave that they require, again giving twice as many days notice as leave being requested of their proposed intentions, e.g. if a worker intends to take ten working days leave, they should give the employer at least 20 days' notice.

If a worker serves notice of their intention to take leave, it is possible for the employer to serve a counter-notice advising them that it will not be possible or they will not be permitted to take leave on the days requested. Such a counter-notice must be served on the worker to a timescale equivalent to the number of days being requested. For example, if the worker is requesting ten days annual leave and has given the required 20 days notice to their employer, then the employer must serve a counter-notice at least ten days before the commencement of the holidays.

The wording of the provisions in Regulation 15 could lead to harsh or unusual results. If, for example, there was one particular day within a period of annual leave of two weeks that the employer did not wish the worker to be absent, then technically the employer need only give one day's notice to the worker that this day's leave is not acceptable – thus leading to an anomalous situation where the employee may already be on annual leave.

For this reason, employers and workers should seek to agree a more amenable method for requesting and granting annual leave which is more fitting to the needs of particular industries.

8. Part-Time Workers

There is nothing contained within the Regulations stipulating the annual leave entitlement for part-time workers. However, the intent of the Regulations as indicated by the Government's DTI guidance is that part-time workers will have an appropriate pro-rata leave entitlement, e.g. a worker working three days a week will be entitled to nine days annual leave rising to 12 days from the 23rd November 1999. In some circumstances, the calculation may not be as straightforward, particularly for workers who work under zero-hour contracts and have been employed in excess of 13 weeks. The most pragmatic solution when calculating these workers' annual leave would be to keep a detailed record of hours worked in each particular month and to notify the workers as and when they accrue annual leave and how it will be calculated. Essentially, even part-time hours over a period of time can be converted into an average days' work thus enabling an employer to calculate a pro-rata entitlement to annual leave.

9. Public and Bank Holidays

The DTI Guidance to the Regulations makes it clear that Public and Bank Holidays are not a statutory entitlement in the United Kingdom. These are days that are either recognised by statute as Public Holidays or they have developed through custom and practice as holidays over a period of time. For example, both Good Friday and Boxing Day are identified within statute law as Bank Holidays, while Christmas Day is a Public Holiday that is recognised as a holiday through custom and practice.

On these days, a worker may receive leave under the terms of their contract of employment. As with any other contractual leave which may be stipulated within the contract, this can be used to discharge an employee's paid annual leave entitlement as stipulated by the Regulations. As a result, where a contract of employment gives employees Public and Bank Holidays off work, these periods of time are paid for and can be deducted from the minimum paid leave entitlement under the Regulations. This means that eight of the 15 paid annual leave days (rising to 20 in November 1999) would be taken up by Public and Bank Holidays.

Therefore, in essence, any contractual right to receive paid holiday on a Bank or Public Holiday need not be in addition to the paid annual leave entitlement under the Regulations.

10. Agricultural Workers

The Agricultural Wages Order framework stipulates arrangements for annual leave for agricultural workers, and the general operation of the leave year. It is the intention of the Regulations that this framework should remain in place Schedule 2 of the Regulations therefore provides for the continuation of the Agricultural Wages Order.

11. Impact of the Paid Annual Leave Provisions

The Regulations introduce the first statutory right to paid annual leave within the United Kingdom. Whilst many workers at present receive a contractual right to paid annual leave often in excess of the minimum statutory entitlement as stipulated by the Regulations, the labour force survey published by the Office for National Statistics in autumn 1996 indicated that there are 2½ million workers who, prior to this legislation, were not entitled to any paid holiday leave.

The introduction of a statutory entitlement to paid annual leave has therefore had a considerable impact upon industries utilising temporary and casual labour, and many organisations will be seeking to review the basis on which this type of work is offered. Traditionally, within such industries as the construction industry for example, paid annual leave has not been awarded to temporary contractors who may work on a site for many months or years at a time for an employer.

There was considerable opposition, most notably from the CBI, to the paid annual leave provisions. David Stockford, Director of Employment Affairs at the Construction Federation, has been quoted as stating that the new paid annual leave provisions will raise labour costs by 2%, thus eating into tight profit margins. There has also been concern raised by the National Farmers' Union for sectors such as horticulture and arable farming due to the significant numbers of casual workers employed within these industries. One estimate puts the total cost to British employers at an extra £470m per year to satisfy the new annual leave provisions.

The provisions contained within Regulation 16 regarding the paid annual leave entitlement provide very little flexibility. The only exception and exclusion to the entitlement are workers who are engaged within excluded sectors and are not afforded the protection of the Regulations generally, as identified by Chapter 1. In many instances, casual workers' rates of pay have been negotiated with the full knowledge of both parties that there will be no entitlement to paid annual leave and the rate of remuneration has been agreed upon accordingly. However, unless it can be clearly established by an employer that a proportion of the rate of pay prior to the 1st October is attributable to annual leave and that workers were receiving payment for any time taken off, then it will be extremely difficult to contend that the normal rate of pay is inclusive of payment for holidays.

A further cost to British industry can be highlighted at Regulation 36 by the introduction of agency workers as a special class of person. Where an agency worker is supplied by an agency to work for another (the principal) under a contract or other arrangement made between the agent and the principal, then this worker will be afforded the protection of the Regulations.

Whoever is responsible for paying the agency worker will be deemed to be the employer for the purposes of the Regulations. In most cases the agency will invoice the company for the work carried out by the individual and a proportion of that money will be passed onto the individual in the form of wages. The agency will therefore be regarded as the employer of that worker and they will need to ensure that the worker is afforded the protection of the Regulations and is provided with their entitlements, including paid annual leave.

As a result, this has lead to agencies passing on the cost of paid annual leave to companies through increased charges.

Employers would be advised to look carefully at their contracts with agencies to ensure that the percentage increase is legitimate and proportionately correct. If the company is seeking to utilise a particular agency worker for a period of time, it ought to be made clear to the agency that it does not expect that worker to exercise his right to paid annual leave during the time that he is working for the company and the contract could legitimately stipulate this.

One option for companies when utilising casual labour would be to ensure that casual workers are employed on fixed-term, 12-week contracts if this is possible and ensuring the continuity of service is broken after the expiry of the contract to avoid the requirement of paying for annual leave for casual workers. Caution should be exercised when utilising casual pools of labour and companies should be aware of the paid annual leave provisions to enable them to meet the costs involved, which, depending on the number of employees employed on a casual basis, could be significant.

CHAPTER 6

Young workers

1. Introduction

The Working Time Regulations 1998 incorporate provisions which were first identified in the Young Workers Directive (Council Directive 94/33/EC). The thrust behind this piece of European legislation lay in the identification of children and adolescents as specific risk groups as a consequence of their inexperience, immaturity and a general absence of awareness of existing or potential risks in the workplace. It was felt that, in view of the nature of the transition from childhood to adult life, the protection of the health and safety of young people needed to be strictly regulated. The implementation of this Directive has subsequently been achieved, in addition to the Working Time Regulations, via the Health and Safety (Young Persons) Regulations 1997, the Children (Protection at Work) Regulations 1998, and regulations relating to work on ships at sea which will be issued in the near future by the Department of the Environment, Transport and the Regions. This Chapter will concentrate primarily on the provisions included in the Working Time Regulations regarding adolescent workers, but will also consider their position with regard to the additional health and safety obligations imposed upon employers.

2. The Meaning of "Young Worker"

The Regulations make certain provisions regarding **young workers**, who are defined as:

"a worker who has attained the age of 15 but not the age of 18 and who, as respects England and Wales, is over compulsory school age... and, as respects Scotland, is over school age".

A young worker is therefore any worker who is above the minimum school leaving age but under 18 years of age. The minimum school leaving age in England and Wales is calculated as the date when he/she has attained the age of 16 or will become 16 between the last Friday in June and the start of the next school year. In Scotland the minimum school leaving age is calculated differently, and a child can leave school either on 31 May, if he or she will attain the age of 16 between 1 March and 30 September in the final school year, or can leave on the first day of the Christmas holiday if he or she will be 16 between 1 October and the last day in February in the final school year. Anyone who works under the age of 16 will be covered by the Children (Protection at Work) Regulations 1998.

3. Working-Time and Night-Time Limits

The working-time limit and the "48-hour week" are equally applicable to both adult workers and young workers. The Regulations make no distinction between the two as far as these provisions are concerned. The same can be said with regard to the night-work limits, and young workers will be subject to working a maximum of eight hours at night for any 24-hour period, averaged out over a 17-week period, just as any adult worker (see Chapter 2).

4. Night Work and Health Assessments

Distinctions are made between the young worker and the adult worker regarding the duties imposed upon employers to carry out health assessments in respect of staff working on nights. Regulation 7(2) states:

"an employer –

(a) *shall not assign a young worker to work during the period between 10:00pm and 6:00am ("the restricted period") unless –*

   (i) *the employer has ensured that the young worker will have the opportunity of a free assessment of his health and capacities before he takes up the assignment; or*

   (ii) *the young worker had an assessment of his health and capacities before being assigned to work during the restricted period on an earlier occasion, and the employer has no reason to believe that the assessment is no longer valid; and*

(b) *shall ensure that each young worker employed by him and assigned to work during the restricted period has the opportunity of a free assessment of his health and capacities at regular intervals of whatever duration may be appropriate in his case."*

This assessment will be more comprehensive compared to the standard assessment of an adult night worker, and an employer will have to take into account the added element of the young worker's "capacities". This will include giving due consideration to issues such as physique, maturity, experience, and competence to undertake duties which may be assigned. These additional factors echo the Council Directive on the Protection of Young Persons at Work, which specifically highlights these factors as being fundamental considerations for the employer in the protection of the young worker.

The employer will therefore have to ensure that due consideration is given to the above factors when assessing any young worker before assigning night work, and ensure that assessments are carried out at regular intervals. There is no guidance as to what would constitute "regular intervals", but to ensure that employers do not breach these provisions, annual assessments would be advisable. However, it is important to note that the employer must look at each young worker and the circumstances surrounding each individual. It may well be the case that some adolescents will require more regular monitoring than others depending on the particular situation. Whatever the time span between the assessments, the cost of carrying out such an assessment must not be borne by the young worker.

Regulation 7(4), however, provides that an employer will not be required to carry out such assessments where the work a young worker is assigned to do is of an exceptional nature. This would cover the situation where it may be necessary for an employer to require a few extra hands on a one-off occasion to undertake some night work, where ordinarily the young worker would work during the daytime.

As is the case for all adult night workers, an employer will be required to keep adequate records to show that the health assessments have been properly offered and performed. Obviously, with regard to the young worker there will be a need not only to show the name of the worker, when the assessment was carried out, and the result of any such assessment, but also to show the additional factors which should have been considered, such as physique and maturity.

5. The Health and Safety (Young Persons) Regulations 1997

These Regulations impose additional factors which must be considered when an employer carries out a health assessment on a young worker. Consideration must also be given to factors such as the fitting out and layout of the workplace and the work station, and how the form, range and use of the work equipment which the adolescent employee may use in the discharge of his duties may affect his or her health and safety. Employers should give thought, therefore, to the danger or degree of strength required to handle a piece of machinery or equipment, or to any other potential difficulties which may be of a problematic nature. They should also ensure that anyone who carries out such assessments familiarises themselves fully with the duties a young worker may have to perform, in order to adequately take account of these factors.

There is also a need for the employer to be aware of the nature, degree and duration of exposure to physical, biological or chemical agents to which a young worker may be subjected. Obviously, the thrust behind this is to ensure that young workers are not exposed to such agents as much as an adult worker might be.

The provisions of the Regulations further provide that an employer should take particular account of the extent to which health and safety training is to be made available to the young worker. This would be of particular relevance where the nature of the work performed involves duties or processes involving exposure to physical, biological or chemical agents.

5.1 After the Assessment

Once the health assessments have been carried out the Health and Safety (Young Persons) Regulations 1997 impose further burdens upon the employer, who will be obliged to provide the employees with comprehensive and relevant information on the risks which have been identified as a result of the assessments. They will further have to state the preventative and/or protective measures which should be taken to alleviate any of these risks.

Furthermore, the Regulations go on to provide that a young worker should not be employed to do work involving certain risks, unless in exceptional circumstances. In determining whether the work involved leaves the adolescent vulnerable to one of the risks detailed below, the employer must take into account the results which have been obtained from risk assessments, as these should be used in a positive fashion and assist in any decision which is to be made. Specifically, the duties which an employer should not expose a young worker to are:

(a)   work which is beyond the physical or psychological capacity of the young worker;

(b) work involving harmful exposure to agents which are toxic or carcinogenic, cause hereditary genetic damage or harm to the unborn child, or which in any other way chronically affect human health;

(c) work involving the harmful exposure to radiation;

(d) work where there is a risk of accidents which, it may reasonably be assumed, cannot be recognised or avoided by young persons owing to their insufficient attention to safety or lack of experience or training;

(e) where there is a risk to health from either extreme cold, heat, noise or vibration.

However, the young worker can be involved in work of the nature described above if it is necessary for his or her training, and a competent person will supervise this training, with the risk being reduced to the lowest level that is reasonably practicable. An employer should therefore take all necessary precautionary steps and give thought to all necessary factors before even considering allowing an adolescent worker to undertake such duties.

6. Rest Periods

The Council Directive on the Protection of Young People at Work specifically provides that, to ensure the health and safety of young people at work, they should be granted a minimum daily, weekly and annual rest period. Accordingly, the Working Time Regulations have introduced measures to implement this provision.

With regard to the daily rest provisions which are contained in Regulation 10(2) and 10(3), young workers are entitled to a rest break for an uninterrupted period of 12 hours in each 24-hour period in which they work. However, this minimum rest period can be split up if periods of work are split up over the day or are of short duration. In other words, it is conceivable that a young worker could be required to work four hours on, four hours off, four hours on, etc. in any 24-hour period. Realistically, this is an unlikely scenario, but it illustrates that the employer does have some flexibility on how the rest break may be taken. However, unlike adult workers, there is virtually no flexibility in the amount of rest which must be taken (see Regulation 27 under "Force majeure").

Regulation 11(3) deals with the minimum weekly rest period a young worker will be entitled to and this states:

"a young worker is entitled to a rest period of not less than 48 hours in each seven-day period during which he works for his employer."

The wording of Regulation 11(3) therefore makes it quite clear that the rest period cannot be averaged out over a two-week period as is the case with adult workers. However, the weekly rest period can be reduced in accordance with Regulation 11(8) which provides:

"The minimum rest period to which a young worker is entitled under paragraph(3) –

(a) *may be interrupted in the case of activities involving periods of work that are split up over the day or are of short duration; and*

(b) *may be reduced where this is justified by technical or organisation reasons, but not to less than 36 consecutive hours."*

Again, as with the daily rest provision, the two-day rest need not be consecutive and can be split up but, unlike the daily rest provisions, the weekly rest period can be reduced. The Guidance from the Department of Trade and Industry states that an employer would have to establish genuine circumstances inherent to the nature of the work or its desired purpose in order to be able to reduce the rest period to 36 hours. It would be wrong for an employer to simply create a situation so as to avoid the young worker's rights under the Regulations.

During the course of the working day, the young worker will, as provided by Regulation 12(4), be entitled to a rest break of 30 minutes if and when more than 4½ hours have been worked, and that this break will be taken consecutively wherever possible. Ideally, the break should be taken away from the workstation. Regulation 12(5) further provides for the situation whereby an adolescent employee may have more than one job. In such circumstances the daily working time is to be aggregated and from this it will then be possible to establish whether the young worker is entitled to a break or not. For example, should a situation exist whereby a young worker works three hours for one employer and then straight away works a further two hours for someone else, then he would be entitled to a 30 minute break. The problem here lies with the actual knowledge of the employer. How are they supposed to know an employee is working elsewhere? The Guidance, however, suggests employers should make enquiries of their young workers to ascertain whether there is any possible entitlement to a rest break and, if so, to ensure that that rest break is being observed.

The provisions as far as annual leave are concerned make no distinction and apply equally to both adult and young workers. These provisions are discussed in Chapter 5.

7. Regulation 27 – "Force Majeure"

With specific regard to Regulation 10(2), regarding a young worker's entitlement to daily rest, and Regulation 12(4), providing for a young worker's entitlement to a rest break, the flexibilities which an adult worker is entitled to and which have been discussed in Chapter 3 regarding break periods, do not apply unless exceptional circumstances exist. A young worker's entitlement to a rest break or daily rest can therefore only be modified or excluded if:

(a) there is no adult worker available to do the work in place of the adolescent;

(b) a situation has arisen due to the occurrence of an unusual or unforeseeable circumstance beyond the employer's control, or there has been an exceptional event, the consequences of which could not have been avoided despite the exercise of all due care by the employer;

(c) the work to be undertaken is of a temporary nature; and

(d) the work to be undertaken is to be performed immediately.

All of the above conditions must apply before a rest break or daily rest break can be reduced or excluded, and clearly the conditions would only apply in a situation that allowed for no other reasonable response. Once the young worker has performed any duties which may be required of him (in circumstances which would allow the above to apply) then the employer must allow for that worker to have the equivalent compensatory rest time within the following three weeks. This compensatory rest time would, therefore, be in addition to any other rest time to which the employee would be entitled.

8. Children (Protection At Work) Regulations 1998

The provisions of the Young Workers Directive (94/33/EC) have also been implemented through amendments to the Children & Young Persons Act 1933 and 1963, and Young Persons (Scotland) Act 1937, with the principal changes relating to age, working time and rest periods.

An amendment to the 1933 Act raised the age at which a child may be engaged in any kind of work from 13 years to 14 years. The exception to this is farming, and a child under 14 may be employed by a parent or guardian in light agricultural or horticultural work. Any employment of this nature must not be on a regular basis and must be limited to occasional help.

Another important change is in the parameters which have been set to define what kind of work a child is permitted to perform. The prohibition against a child doing "work likely to injure him/her" has now been replaced with a prohibition against anything other than "light work". "Light work" is defined at the newly inserted Section 18 (2A) as:

"Work which on account of the inherent nature of the tasks which it involves and the particular conditions under which they are performed –

- (a) *is not likely to be harmful to the safety, health or development of children; and*

- (b) *is not such as to be harmful to their attendance at school or to their participation in work experience in accordance with Section 560 of the Education Act 1996, or their capacity to benefit from the instruction received or, as the case may be, the experience gained."*

Any child of 15 years and over, with regard to daily working time, is not permitted to work for more than eight hours on any day upon which that child is not required to attend at school, or any day which is not a Sunday. Weekly working hours must not exceed 35, again so long as the child is not supposed to attend school during that week. The same is applicable for a child under the age of 15, except that the daily working limit is five hours and the weekly working limit is 25 hours.

With regard to rest periods, any child must not work for more than four hours in any day without a rest break of one hour. The new provisions also provide that during school holidays in any one year, which runs from

1st January, a child has at least one two week period free from any employment whatsoever.

The 1933 Act has also been amended to extend the definition of activities which are prohibited from being performed abroad for payment, in the absence of a local authority licence. The definition now includes children who play sport or model for payment, and any child doing so will be required to obtain a local authority licence if any payments are to be made (save for reasonable expenses). Amendments to the 1963 Act have also extended the requirement to hold a local authority licence for children taking part in public performances of a sporting or modelling nature where payment is to be made, whether such payment is made to the child or to someone else.

CHAPTER 7

Enforcement and remedies

1. Who are the Enforcers?

The Regulations create a hybrid enforcement system, using both the criminal law and enhanced employment protection rights, enforceable by employment tribunals. Part IV of the Regulations details the enforcement mechanisms and remedies. Where the Regulations give a worker an entitlement, and the worker is prevented by the employer from exercising that entitlement, then the worker can complain to an employment tribunal (see Part 4 below). However, the Government also identifies with the objectives of the EC directive and, where the Regulations impose limits on working time and provisions relating to night work and record keeping, these matters will be enforced in the same way as existing health and safety legislation by inspectors from the Health and Safety Executive and local authority environmental health officers. This enforcement is underpinned by the criminal law.

Prior to providing details of the specific offences under the Regulations and the available enforcement powers, therefore, it is important to place the Regulations in the context of other health and safety legislation and have a knowledge of the Health and Safety Commission's policy on enforcement.

2. The Health and Safety Commission's Policy Statement on Enforcement

The Health and Safety Commission (HSC) aims to protect the health and safety of workers and others, namely the public, who may be exposed to risks from work activities. Bearing in mind that the Regulations stipulate the maximum weekly working time and provisions in respect of night work and record keeping, the Health and Safety Executive (the enforcement arm of the HSC) when deciding whether or not to prosecute employers for breach of the Regulations will be influenced by whether the employers have exposed workers to unacceptable risks through the failure to comply. The enforcing authorities must seek to secure compliance, but HSE and local authority inspectors are also available for information, advice and support.

There are many guidance documents on health and safety law available to employers. Ultimately, if the relevant enforcement authority takes the view that employers are acting in breach of the Regulations and contrary to health and safety law generally, then the HSC's view is that there should be a quick and effective response.

The main legal obligations placed on employers and the dominant piece of legislation governing health and safety law is the Health and Safety at Work Act 1974. Sections 2 to 6 of the Act specify the general duties of employers. The overriding duty at section 2(1) is that it shall be the duty of every employer to ensure so far as is reasonably practicable the health, safety and welfare at work of all employees.

This section should be considered in conjunction with the new Regulations. It should be noted that if an employer breaches the Regulations, then the employer could also be in breach of the general duty under Section 2(1) of the Health and Safety at Work Act 1974.

The Health and Safety Executive's principles of enforcement are:

1. proportionality;

2. consistency;

3. targeting;

4. transparency.

2.1 Proportionality

When considering the appropriate enforcement action to take for breaches of the law, the HSE will seek to ensure that the enforcement action is proportionate to any risks to health and safety, and will consider the gravity of any breach. However, when considering the seriousness of the breach and what form of action ought to have been taken by the employer in safeguarding the health and safety of employees, the HSE will have due regard to relevant good practice and whether or not it was followed.

If one applies the principle of proportionality to the policing of the Working Time Regulations it will mean that the HSE will assess what impact a breach of the Regulations has had on a particular worker when considering prosecution. Especially during the infancy stage of the Regulations it is likely that the enforcing authority's position on the Regulations will be one of reacting to incidents at particular companies.

For example, if an employee is subject to an injury within the workplace and the HSE are making general enquiries into the accident, then they may ask to see a company's records to ascertain how many hours the employee has worked during the preceding weeks. If there are no records, or the records indicate the individual has worked excessive hours with inadequate rest periods, the enforcing authority may be inclined to conclude that these are influential factors which have contributed to the accident.

With regard to relevant good practice, many companies are taking the Regulations very seriously and implementing policies on working time and drawing up either collective or workforce agreements to utilise particular derogations. This has to be considered good practice and if a company has chosen to ignore the passing of the Regulations and is found to be in breach of them, this is likely to bear heavily upon whether or not the HSE choose to prosecute.

2.2 Consistency

The HSE endeavour to achieve consistency in the way that they approach enforcing issues and the advice tendered.

2.3 Transparency

Transparency is to ensure that employers and duty holders understand what is expected of them and what they should expect from the enforcing authorities. It is important for employers to know what is expected from them if an inspector calls, and what rights of complaint are open to them.

2.4 Targeting

This is used by the enforcing authorities to target those activities which give rise to the most serious risk, or where hazards are least well controlled. This is obviously of less importance when dealing with obligations under the Regulations unless it can be seen that employees are working such excessive hours that there is a very serious risk of injury to either the workers or members of the public, for example.

Ultimately, however, enforcing authorities will use their discretion on whether or not to initiate a prosecution. Prosecutions will be commenced if the enforcing authority believe that there is a need to draw general attention to the necessity for compliance with the law and the maintenance of standards. They will also consider the gravity of the offence and the general record of the offender.

3. Criminal Enforcement

As previously stated, the Health and Safety Executive and local authorities will be predominately concerned with enforcing the limits specified by the Regulations – the 48-hour week and the provisions on length of night work, for example. This enforcement is underpinned by the criminal law and breaches of the relevant Regulations set out below are criminal offences. Prosecutions are therefore heard by the Magistrates' Courts or the Crown Courts.

Regulation 28 compels the HSE to make adequate arrangements for the enforcement of the relevant requirement, except to the extent that a local authority is made responsible for enforcement. The HSE will be responsible for enforcement in relation to factories, mines, quarries, chemical plants, nuclear installations, building sites, fairgrounds, schools and hospitals. However, retail premises, offices, hotels, catering, sports, leisure and consumer services will be the responsibility of local authority officers. The specific responsibilities of the HSE and local authorities are to ensure compliance with the following provisions:

(a) the employer's duty to take all reasonable steps to comply with the maximum weekly working time limit (Regulation 4 – see Chapter 2);

(b) the employer's duty to take all reasonable steps to ensure that night-work limits are complied with, both in relation to normal night working hours and hazardous night work (Regulation 6 – see Chapter 4);

(c) to ensure that employers comply with their obligations to provide the opportunity for free health assessments on a regular basis for adult night workers, and health and capacity assessments for young workers (Regulation 7 (1) and (2) – see Chapter 4);

(d) to comply with the duty to transfer night workers who are no longer capable of performing night work to day work, wherever possible (Regulation 7 – see Chapter 4);

(e) to comply with the provisions to provide adequate rest breaks where work is monotonous pursuant to a particular pattern of work which could affect the health and safety of the workers (Regulation 8 – see Chapter 3);

(f) employers are also under a duty to keep records of weekly working hours, the length of night work and the provisions on free health assessments (Regulation 9). In addition, inspectors will also have power to inspect employers' records in relation to workers who have signed an opt-out agreement (Regulation 5);

(g) to ensure that the compensatory rest provisions are satisfied (Regulation 24).

3.1 Penalties

Prior to considering financial penalties, an HSE or local authority inspector may consider whether or not an employer is in breach of any of the above provisions and, if so, issue an "improvement notice" requiring the employer to remedy the breach. It will be a criminal offence if the employer fails to comply with the improvement notice. In accordance with health and safety law, if the employer obstructs an inspector or interferes with the investigations or provides false information, then this will also constitute an offence.

Regulation 29 stipulates that if an employer is found guilty of a criminal offence under any of the above provisions, the employer will be liable to pay a fine, which on summary conviction in a Magistrates Court, will be subject to a statutory maximum of currently, £5,000. If the employer is convicted on indictment before the Crown Court, which is likely to be only in very serious and rare cases, then the fine will be unlimited.

4. Employment Tribunal Complaints

In addition to the potential criminal liability explained above, individual workers are entitled to bring claims before an employment tribunal if their employers breach the Regulations – by preventing them from exercising their entitlements to rest an/or annual leave, for example. The criteria which need to be satisfied to bring particular claims before an employment tribunal for breach of the Regulations are examined below.

4.1 Regulation 30

Employers who deny workers the following entitlements risk claims before an employment tribunal:

Regulation 10 (1 and 2)	daily rest
Regulation 11 (1, 2 and 3)	weekly rest
Regulation 12 (1 and 4)	rest break
Regulation 13 (1)	annual leave
Regulations 14 (2) and 16 (1)	pay for annual leave, both during employment and on termination of employment
Regulation 24	compensatory rest provisions
Regulation 25	compensatory rest for young workers employed within the armed forces who are not provided with compensatory rest when they are not able to take a rest period
Regulation 27	compensatory rest for young workers required to work at a time that would otherwise be a rest period due to unusual or unforeseeable circumstances (beyond the employer's control or as a result of exceptional events) where the work is of a temporary nature and must be performed immediately.

4.2 Regulation 31 – Unlawful Detriment

This Regulation inserts additional sections into the Employment Rights Act 1996. For example, section 45A states that a worker has the right not to be subjected to any detriment by any act, or any deliberate failure to act by his employer on the grounds that the worker:

a) refused (or proposed to refuse) to comply with a requirement which the employer either proposed to impose or actually imposed in contravention of the Regulations;

b) proposed to refuse or refused to forego a right conferred on him by those Regulations;

c) failed to sign a workforce agreement for the purposes of varying the Regulations, or to enter into or agree to vary or extend any other agreement with the employer which is provided for in the Regulations;

d) either being a workforce representative or a candidate at such an election or generally performing any functions or activities as a workforce representative or a candidate;

e) bringing proceedings against an employer to enforce a right or entitlement granted by the Regulations;

f) alleging that an employer has infringed such a right.

With regards to (e) and (f) it does not matter whether or not the worker has the right or whether the right has been infringed, it only matters that both the claim to the right and the fact that it has been infringed were made in good faith. If an employee or worker can show the employer that he/she believes that the employer has infringed rights under the Regulations, and can then establish that he/she is being subjected to a detriment as a result of bringing that to the attention of the employer, then this will be sufficient to establish a successful claim under (f) above.

A detriment for the purposes of the Employment Rights Act 1996 would include actions such as denying promotion, bringing unjustified disciplinary action, refusing opportunities for training, reducing pay, and any other adverse treatment.

In cases where the adverse treatment is dismissal, one important proviso contained within Regulation 31 relates to where the complainant is an employee rather than a worker under the broader definition contained within the Regulations. If an employee, the complaint must not be made under Section 45A but under Section 101(A) – which relates to automatically unfair dismissal – which was inserted by Regulation 32 (1) of the Regulations. The exception to this is where the dismissal arises only by virtue of a fixed-term contract expiring without its being renewed, and the employee has waived his/her right to claim unfair dismissal in these circumstances. (It should be noted, however, that such waivers are due to be abolished, when relevant provisions of the Employment Relations Bill come into force).

4.3 Regulation 32 – Automatically Unfair Dismissal

Regulation 32 inserts a new provision into the Employment Rights Act 1996. Under Section 101(A) of the Employment Rights Act 1996, an employee who is dismissed shall be regarded as unfairly dismissed if the principal reason for the dismissal is that the employee:

a) proposed to refuse or refused to comply with an instruction from the employer which would be in contravention of the Regulations;

b) proposed to refuse or refused to forego a right conferred on him by the Regulations;

c) failed to sign a workforce agreement or to enter into or agree to vary or extend any other agreement with the employer provided for in the Regulations;

d) is a workforce representative or is a candidate in an election to become such a representative, or proposed to perform or performed any functions or activities as a representative or candidate.

A finding of unfair dismissal is automatic once the tribunal has found one of the above to be the principal reason for the dismissal. In other words, it is irrelevant whether or not the employer acted reasonably under section 98(4) of the Employment Rights Act 1996 – by following the correct procedure, for example.

The Regulations also insert a new Section 105 (4A). This provides that if an employer dismisses an employee on the grounds of redundancy, and the employee contends that the dismissal was automatically unfair pursuant to Section 101A, the dismissal will be found to be automatically unfair if other employees in the same undertaking holding similar positions were not also made redundant.

In addition, Section 104 of the Employment Rights Act 1996 is amended by Regulation 32(2), and now ensures that an employee will be regarded as being automatically unfairly dismissed if the employee is dismissed for bringing proceedings against the employer to enforce a statutory right under the Regulations, or for alleging that the employer has infringed such a right.

As with Section 45A (e) and (f), it is immaterial whether or not the employee actually has the right or whether the right has actually been infringed, providing that the employee's claim is made in good faith.

4.4 Qualifying Period

Unlike normal claims for unfair dismissal – which at the time of writing require two years' qualifying service before an employee is statutorily entitled to bring such an action – a claim under Section 101A requires no qualifying period and there is no upper age limit for bringing a claim. Employees therefore have unfair dismissal rights under the Regulations from day one of employment and the rights are not affected if they are over normal retiring age.

It should be noted, however, that it is proposed under the forthcoming fairness at work legislation to reduce the qualifying period for normal unfair dismissal actions from two years' service to one year's service. This is due to come into force on 1st June 1999. It should also be remembered that Section 101A applies only to employees and not to the broader category of workers. A worker's form of redress would be under Section 45A (see part 4.2 above).

4.5 Time Limits

As with normal employment tribunal claims, a claim must be presented to the tribunal within three months of the allegedly unlawful action. With regard to Regulation 30, the three-month limit will begin on the date that the exercise of the alleged entitlement should have been permitted. For members of the armed forces, special rules apply which require them to utilise internal service redress procedures before embarking on an employment tribunal claim. Therefore, for members of the armed forces, the time limit for a tribunal complaint is six months from the date of the action complained of.

Regulation 31 – unlawful detriment claims – is again subject to the three-month rule. The only difference here, however, is that the three months begin to run from the last such act of the employer if there are a series of acts or failures on the part of the employer. The time limit for an unfair dismissal complaint in accordance with Regulation 32 is three months from the effective date of termination.

As with all complaints presented to an employmen t tribunal, if there are grounds for the tribunal to be satisfied that it was not reasonably practicable for a complaint to be presented within the specified three-month time limit, then the complaint may be presented within such further period as the tribunal considers reasonable.

5. Remedies

5.1 Regulation 30

A well-founded complaint under Regulation 30 (see Part 4.1 above) will require the tribunal to make a declaration to that effect. The tribunal may also make an award of compensation, the amount of which shall be such as the tribunal considers just and equitable in all the circumstances, having regard to:

(a) the employer's default in refusing to permit the worker to exercise the right;

(b) any loss sustained by the worker which is attributable to the matters complained of.

There is no limit on the amount of compensation which may be awarded.

A specific complaint for non-payment of statutory holiday or payment in lieu of holidays upon termination will mean that the tribunal will order that the employer pays the due amount.

5.2 Unlawful Detriment

The same remedies apply to a successful complaint under Section 45A (unlawful detriment – see part 4.2 above). The tribunal, when considering what amount is just and equitable will take into account actual losses attributable to the employer's actions, together with any expenses reasonably incurred. As in all assessments for compensation, the tribunal will have due regard to whether or not the worker has been able to mitigate the loss or whether he/she contributed to the situation in any way.

5.3 Unfair Dismissal

Where a tribunal makes a finding of automatic unfair dismissal under Section 101A of the Employment Rights Act 1996, it is first under a duty to consider whether or not it is practicable to reinstate or re-engage the employee.

5.3.1 Reinstatement

Reinstatement is defined by the Employment Rights Act 1996 as *"an order that the employer shall treat the [employee] in all respects as if he had not been dismissed"*. When deciding whether to grant such orders tribunals must consider:

(a) whether the employee wants to be reinstated;

(b) whether such reinstatement is practicable for the employer (for example, it may not be practical where it will lead to industrial unrest or over-manning);

(c) where the employee caused or contributed to his or her own dismissal, whether the reinstatement is just.

Having made a decision reinstate, the resulting order must state:

(a) the amount of money to be paid to the employee in reimbursement for the benefits and income lost as a result of the dismissal from the date of termination to the date of reinstatement;

(b) the rights and privileges which must be restored to the employee, including seniority and pension rights;

(c) the date on which the order must be complied with and, if applicable, that the employee is to benefit from any improvements in the terms and conditions of employment from which the employee would have benefited had he or she not had been dismissed.

5.3.2 Re-engagement

If the tribunal decides not to make an order for reinstatement, it must consider whether to make an order for re-engagement, which defines the Employment Rights Act 1996 as: *"an order, on such terms as the tribunal may decide, that the [employee] be engaged by the employer, or by a successor of the employer or by an associated employer, in employment comparable to that from which he was dismissed or other suitable employment"*.

When deciding whether to order re-engagement and thereafter setting the terms of it, the tribunal must consider the wishes of the employee, and whether the employer's compliance is practicable. Having done so, the new terms must be, so far as reasonably practicable, as favourable (but not substantially more so) as if the employee had been reinstated as opposed to re-engaged, unless the tribunal considers that the employee contributed in some way to his or her own dismissal. Finally, the order must include all of the items required in a reinstatement order, plus:

(a) the identity of the employer;

(b) the nature of the employment;

(c) the remuneration for that employment.

The level of unfair dismissal compensation is currently capped under the normal principles. At the time of writing, the maximum basic award for a finding of unfair dismissal amounts to £6,600 (based on 20 years' service, aged 41 or over, at the maximum gross weekly wage of £220)

5.3.3 Basic Award

The basic award is calculated using the following formula:

$$\text{Number of full years' continuous service (capped at 20)} \times (\text{Age factor} \times \text{gross weekly pay (capped at £220)})$$

The age factors are as follows:

0.5 where the years have been worked while the employee was under 22 years old;

1.0 where the years have been worked while the employee was aged between 22 and under 41;

1.5 where the years have been worked while the employee was aged 41 or over.

It should also be noted that if the continuous service spans more than one age category, separate calculations will have to be carried out in respect of the years worked in each age category and a total obtained by adding them together.

Having calculated the basic award the tribunal will consider whether it should be reduced on any of the following three grounds:

(a) if the employee is over 64 years old at the date of termination the basic award is reduced by 1/12th for each month the employee has worked since turning 64, thus the basic award will be nil if the employee is 65 or over at the date of termination;

(b) if the reason for the dismissal was redundancy, any redundancy payment made will be deducted from the basic award;

(c) the tribunal has discretion to reduce the award where it considers it to be just and equitable, taking into account the employee's conduct prior to the dismissal, or any unreasonable refusal by the employee to accept an offer of reinstatement.

In addition, the employee would be entitled to:

a) a compensatory award (to compensate the employee for the losses sustained in consequence of the dismissal, in so far as those losses are attributable to the employer), which is currently capped at £12,000;

b) an additional award where the employer fails to comply with an order to reinstate or re-engage the employee, in circumstances where compliance was practicable, amounting to between 13–26 weeks' pay, ie, £2,860–£5,720.

It is important to note, however, that the present ceiling on the compensatory award will be removed as soon as the forthcoming fairness at work legislation (the Employment Relations Bill) becomes law, anticipated to be some during 1999. The new maximum compensatory award limit will be £50,000. This figure will be subject to yearly adjustment in accordance with the retail prices index, once the Employment Relations Bill becomes law.

It is also worthy of note that, as well as the statutory maxima for both the basic award and the compensatory award, where the dismissal is for trade union, health and safety or employee representative reasons, there is also a minimum basic award of £2,900. If, therefore, the unfair dismissal is on the ground of the employee's functions or activities as a workforce representative then the employee will be entitled to a minimum basic award of £2,900.

5.4 Regulation 35 – Restrictions on Contracting Out

It is not possible to enter into a contract or an agreement (whether or not the contract is a contract of employment) to exclude the application or attempt to limit the applicability of any of the Regulations. It is also not possible for workers to waive their rights to bring claims under the Regulations before an employment tribunal, except as explained below.

The only exceptions are where the parties enter into a conciliated settlement through the services of ACAS or a valid compromise agreement. The conditions governing compromise agreements are set out in Section 203(3) of the Employment Rights Act 1996 (duplicated in Regulation 35(3)), and are as follows:

1. the Agreement must be in writing and relate to a particular complaint;

2. the worker must have received advice from a relevant independent advisor in accordance with the Employment Rights (Dispute Resolution) Act 1998, i.e. a qualified lawyer or an accredited trade union or Citizens Advice Bureau representative;

3. the advisor must have a valid contract of insurance or an indemnity covering the risk of negligent advice;

4. the agreement must identify the adviser;

5. the agreement must state that the conditions regulating compromise agreements under the Regulations are satisfied.

Civil Court Enforcement

As highlighted in Chapter 2, in the case of *Barber and others v. R J B Mining UK Limited* (3rd March 1999), the High Court decided that Regulation 4(1) creates a contractual right which may be enforced by employees in the civil courts. Regulation 4(1) provides that a worker's working time, including overtime, in any reference period which is applicable in his case shall not exceed an average of 48 hours for each seven days.

Furthermore, the High Court decided that this right exists separately from Regulation 4(2), which imposes a duty on employers to take reasonable steps to ensure compliance with the 48-hour limit, and is enforceable by the Health and Safety Executive or local authorities (see Chapter 2).

In the Barber case, the High Court declared that pit deputies, who had already worked more than an average of 48 hours per week during the previous 17 weeks, need not work again until their average working hours fell within the Regulation 4(1) limit. In the court's view, Parliament clearly intended that the contract of employment should be read so as to provide that an employee should work no more than an average of 48 hours per week during the applicable reference period, and this was therefore a mandatory requirement that applied to all employment contracts. The employees were therefore entitled to refuse to work until their average hours came within the specified limits. It is also worth noting that the employees' possible motives for the proceedings (which were brought in the context on an on-going wage dispute) were deemed irrelevant.

The deputies were not, however, entitled to an injunction restraining R J B Limited from requiring them to work until this time, or an injunction prohibiting R J B Limited from dismissing them or subjecting them to any detriment for refusing to work. If the employees suffered any detriment as a result of their refusal to exceed the limits specified by Regulation 4(1), they would have their rights to claim to an employment tribunal under Section 45(A) of the Employment Rights Act 1996 (see part 4.2 above).

Changing Contracts of Employment

So far, this book has reviewed the legal requirements imposed by the Regulations, the exclusions and derogations conferring flexibility, and the enforcement procedures and remedies, to deal with breaches. Employers should therefore be able to work out whether their working arrangements comply, and they should seek legal advice if they are at all uncertain. If they do not meet the requirements of the Regulations in some respect, the first question is whether or not there are flexibilities which may assist. For example, would a workforce or collective agreement in the appropriate terms enable the employer to vary the Regulations' requirements? Alternatively, do any of Regulation 21 special circumstances apply?

Even if shift patterns or working hours are compliant, is the employer happy with the annual leave notification procedures introduced by the Regulations? In the absence of existing contractual arrangements, these will apply to regulate the statutory minimum leave under the Regulations – if not any excess leave – and may, for example, not give an employer sufficient notice of an employee's intention to take leave.

If, having considered these issues, an employer concludes that its working arrangements need changing, how can this be achieved? It is straightforward where the Regulations confer new rights, for example paid holiday entitlement for casual staff. Simple notification of new rights will no doubt be gratefully received! On the other hand, altering hours of work, especially for employed staff, may be more difficult. Following the Barber case it is a mandatory requirement in all employment contracts that no employee should work more than an average of 48 hours per week during the applicable reference period. Consider a contract for four 12-hour shifts per week with an obligation to perform compulsory overtime, if required. In this case, the mandatory requirement will supersede the obligation to work overtime, unless the individuals concerned agree to opt out of the 48-hour maximum working week provisions. Those who wish to continue to perform overtime, therefore, should be asked to opt out. If insufficient numbers wish to opt out, the employer will need to make alternative arrangements to cover the overtime work, such as the use of agency labour, or to increase staff numbers.

The night-work averages cannot be avoided by individual opt-out, only by collective or workforce agreement or the existence of special circumstances. Non-compliant night shift patterns (see for example chapter 4 part 9.3) are, therefore, one example where formal contractual variations may be necessary; simply imposing compliant working arrangements, particularly if they result in the loss of pay to which the employees are currently contractually entitled, should be viewed with caution. Although arguably existing working arrangements are unlawful, this does not necessarily render then ineffective or voidable. It could be, for example, that they are perfectly compliant up to a certain point in the reference period, provided the employees then have an extra day or two off but this may not be the most appropriate solution from an employer's point of view.

The employer should therefore firstly review which aspects of its working arrangements do not comply and formulate proposals to remedy the situation. Once the proposals for changes have been formulated, the next step is to review the existing contracts of employment, to see whether or not they contain sufficient flexibility to give scope to make the required changes. If so, provided the employer's changes do not go beyond what the flexibility clause allows (and the clause will be construed narrowly), then the employer will commit no breach of contract by imposing the change. The employer should, however, take care of two points: first, that the decision to vary is based on reasonable or sufficient grounds and, secondly, that the employer exercises their rights to vary under the contract in such a way that trust and confidence between employer and employee is not destroyed. On the first point, there is little doubt that a decision to vary terms to ensure compliance with the Regulations, will be considered reasonable grounds and, for the second part, communication and consultation will be of vital importance.

Where the contract does not allow this flexibility, changes can only be effected lawfully in one of two ways:

(a) by consent. The express consent of an employee to a variation of his/her contract (best evidenced by them signing a written document setting out the variation and their acceptance in full) is the most desirable solution to achieve effective changes of terms and conditions. Where a recognised trade union has collective bargaining rights for all terms and conditions, their agreement to variations of terms can be said to be binding on the employees they represent, provided the employees' contracts incorporate such collective agreements and the union is acting as the employees' agent. To avoid complications, however, individual acceptance should always be obtained, although in most cases the agreement of the union will make this easier.

It is important to note, however, that although a workforce agreement negotiated by employee representatives can modify or exclude the application of the Regulations in some respects, they do not have collective bargaining rights as such and it would not be advisable for an employer to rely on a workforce agreement to vary individual terms and conditions of employment.

(b) by dismissal and re-employment on the new terms. If express consent is not obtained, dismissal on due notice, coupled with an offer of re-employment on new terms, is the one remaining option to secure effective variation. Those with one or more year's continuous employment at the date of dismissal, however, will be eligible to claim unfair dismissal, even where they accept re-employment on the new terms. If successful in a claim for unfair dismissal and they remain in employment, the employee would be entitled to a basic award and compensation broadly to make up any difference between the old and new terms and conditions for a specified period of time.

To defend such claims, the employer would need to:

(a) establish a sound business case for seeking to effect the changes (to establish some other substantial reason (SOSR) as the potentially fair reason for the dismissal); and

(b) on the basis that this reason is sufficient to justify the dismissals in all the circumstances, adopt a fair procedure in effecting such dismissals. A fair procedure will include both individual and collective consultation, the latter of which is required by the Trade Union and Labour Relations (Consolidation) Act 1992 (Section 188(1)), if 20 or more employees are proposed to be dismissed within a period of 90 days or less.

With regard to SOSR, there is little doubt that a need to vary working arrangements which do not comply with the Regulations will amount to an SOSR and hence a potentially fair reason for the dismissal. In terms of the sufficiency of this reason for dismissing, however, the employment tribunal will explore alternatives to dismissal, including the flexibility available under the Regulations, in determining whether or not dismissal was reasonable in all the circumstances. It is therefore important that, during any period of consultation, all options are explored with the employees and their representatives before changes are imposed in this way.

The collective consultation obligations under the 1992 Act bite in a redundancy situation, but "redundancy" in this context means a dismissal for a reason not relating to the individual concerned, or for a number of reasons, all of which are not so related. A dismissal for a business reason – to effect a change to terms and conditions to ensure compliance with the Regulations – would fall within this definition. In short, they impose minimum consultation time limits and specific obligations to consult with the appropriate representatives, which are either representatives of recognised trade unions or elected employee representatives. The consultation time limits are as follows:

(a) at least 90 days before the first dismissal takes effect where the employer is proposing to dismiss more than 100 employees at any one establishment within a period of 90 or less;

(b) in any other case where consultation is required (i.e. where between 20 and 100 dismissals are proposed), consultation must begin at least 30 days before the first of those dismissals takes effect.

A full explanation of the collective consultation obligations in these circumstances is outside the scope of this book. However, it is clear that where the Regulations are concerned, collective consultation will potentially take on a dual role; not only is it necessary to effect required changes in a lawful manner if dismissals are ultimately required, but it may also lead to a consensus to the changes or to the negotiation of an appropriate workforce or collective agreement under the Regulations, to avoid the need for dismissals or even the changes proposed.

APPENDIX A

Working Time Regulations Consent Form

I understand that I am not permitted to work in excess of a 48 hour week (averaged over a reference period of 17 weeks) unless I sign to the effect that I am prepared to do so.

Please tick whichever statement applies to you

I agree that this limit should *not* apply in my case.
I agree that I can terminate this agreement by giving [   ] written notice. ☐

or

I do not work in excess of the limit and I agree that it should apply to me.
I understand I can opt out of this limit at any time by signing a further consent form. ☐

I will be recording my working time using the following method (please tick):

        Overtime Records   ☐

        Manual Time Sheets   ☐

SIGNATURE:
....

FULL NAME (capitals please):
....

DEPT
....

DATE:
....

      Please return this form to[   ], Human Resources Department BY [DATE]

INDEX

48-hour working week 13-30
  17-week reference period 19
  26-week reference period 20, 21-4
  52-week reference period 20-1
  average calculation *see*
    calculation of 48-hour average
  employers' duties 13
    breach of 30
  enforcement 13
  excluded workers 15
  measurement *see* measurement
    of 48-hour limit
  opt-out *see* opt-out of 48-hour
    working week
  penalties for breach 13, 30
  records *see* record keeping,
    48-hour working week
  unmeasured working time 15-16
  workers covered 14-15
  workers with more than
    one job 25-6
  workers' rights 30
  working time
    agreements 18-19
    basic definition 17
    break times 18
    home working 18
    on-call time 17, 18
    travel time 17
  young workers 72
accidents 23, 38
accounts staff 23
agency workers 6, 7
  holiday entitlement 69
Agricultural Wages Order 67
agriculture 6, 22, 23, 38, 51, 67
  young workers 78
air workers 2, 7
airport workers 22, 38, 51
ambulance service 8
annual hours, night workers 47-8

annual leave
  employment tribunal
    complaints 86
  notification procedures 95-6
  payment 86
  young workers 77
annualised hours contracts,
  holiday entitlement 63
armed forces 6, 8
automatically unfair dismissal,
  redress procedures 89
average working hours 95

bank holidays 67
*Barber and others v RJB Mining
  (UK) Ltd* 13, 30, 94-5, 96
breach of provisions
  criminal offence, penalties 85
  improvement notice 85
  penalties 85
  see also employment
    tribunal complaints
break times
  and 48-hour working week 18
  see also rest periods
building sites 84

calculation of 48-hour
  average 24-5
  excluded days 24-5
  holiday leave 24
  sick leave 24
  voluntary overtime 24
caretakers 38
casual workers
  12-week contracts 69
  holiday entitlement 68
  measurement of 48-hour limit 20
catering 84
chemical plants 84
Children (Protection at Work)
  Regulations 1998 71, 78-9

churches, workers officiating at religious ceremonies	16, 37, 50
cinematographic production	22, 38, 51
civil protection services	22, 38
cleaning staff	39
collective agreements	
definition	10
holiday entitlement	65
night workers	53
rest period entitlements	40
to extend reference period	20-1, 23
compensatory rest	39
employment tribunal complaints	86
enforcement	85
night workers	53-4
variation of rest period entitlements	40-1
consumer services	84
continuity of service	22, 38
contracting-out, restriction	94
contracts of employment, changing	95-9
by dismissal and re-employment on new terms	97-8
collective consultation obligations	98
employee's consent	97
trade union consent	97
workforce agreement	97
Crown employees	6
daily rest	31, 34
employment tribunal complaints	86
night workers	46-7
date Regulations, effective from	1, 4
detriment	95
definition	87
disabled person, definition	58
disabled workers	
employer's obligations	58-9
night work	58-9
distribution	22
dock workers	22, 38, 51
doctors in training	2, 8
domestic service	15, 52
DTI, *Regulatory Guidance*	4
EC, Social Charter	2
EC Directives	2-3
exempt workers	2
UK challenge	2-3
ECJ ruling	3
Working Time Directive	2
UK consultation documents	4
Young Workers Directive	2, 3-4, 71
electricity industry	22, 38, 51
employers' records, enforcement	85
employment agencies, workers supplied through	7, 14-15
Employment Rights Act 1996	88, 95
employment tribunal	
complaints	81, 85-93
ACAS	94
annual leave	86
payment	86
compensatory rest	86
compromise agreements	94
daily rest	86
remedies	90
unfair dismissal	90-3
unlawful detriment	90
rest breaks	86
unfair dismissal	87, 88-9
qualifying period	89
remedies	90-3
time limits	89-90
unlawful detriment	86-7, 89, 90, 95
weekly rest	86
see also breach of provisions	
enforcement	
civil enforcement	94-95
compensatory rest	85
criminal	84-5
employers' records	85
health assessments	84
Health and Safety Commission policy	81-4
Health and Safety Executive's responsibilities	84
improvement notice	85

local authorities'
  responsibilities 84
maximum weekly working
  time limit 84
night-work limits 84
rest breaks for monotonous
  work 84-5
Environmental Health Officer,
  inspection of records re. hours
  worked 28
exceptional events 23, 38
excluded workers 7-8

factories 84
fairgrounds 84
family workers 16, 37, 50
farming *see* agriculture
fire service 8
"Francovich" claims 5

gas industry 22, 38, 51
government, claims for damages
  against by workers 5

health assessments
  enforcement 84
  night workers 56-7
  young workers 73-4
health and safety, employers'
  obligations 82
Health and Safety at Work
  Act 1974 82
Health and Safety Commission,
  enforcement policy 81-4
Health and Safety Executive 81
  enforcement principles
    consistency 83
    proportionality 82-3
    targeting 83-4
    transparency 83
  enforcement responsibilities 84
  inspection of records re. hours
    worked 28
Health and Safety (Young Persons)
  Regulations 1997 71, 73-5
holiday entitlement 61-9
  agency workers 69
  agricultural workers 67

annualised hours contracts 63
calculation of 48-hour average 24
carrying proportion forward
  to following year 62
casual workers 68, 69
collective agreement 65
commencement of leave year 62
  with effect from 23.11.99 61
impact of paid leave provisions
  on British industry 68-9
leave year 23.11.98 to
  23.11.99 61
part-time workers 66-7
payment
  holiday credit schemes 65
  normal week's pay 64-5
payment in lieu 63
  upon termination 63-4
public and bank holidays 67
qualifying period 61-2
relevant agreement 65
when leave may be taken 62-3,
  65-6
worker beginning during
  leave year 62
home working 33
  and 48-hour working week 18
hospitals 22, 38, 51, 84
hotels 84
House of Commons and House
  of Lords staff 6
household refuse collection 22,
  38, 51

industries which cannot be
  interrupted on technical
  grounds 22, 38, 51
inland waterway transport 2, 7
interpretation of regulations,
  "purposively" 5

lake transport 2, 7
leisure services 84
light work, definition 78
local authorities, enforcement
  responsibilities 84
lunch, working through 18
lunch breaks 34

Index **105**

lunches/evening meals on
  business   18, 33

managing executives   16, 36, 37, 50
measurement of 48-hour limit   19-24
  17-week reference period   19
  26 week reference period   20
    circumstances when
      applicable   21-4
  up to 52 week reference
    period   20-1
  workers employed for less
    than 17 weeks   19-20
mines   84
monotonous work, rest
  breaks   35-6, 53, 84-5

night time
  definition   43-4
  relevant agreement re hours   43-4
night workers   43-60
  annual hours   47-8
  collective and workforce
    agreements   53
  compensatory rest   53-4
  daily rest breaks   46-7
  definition   44, 45-6
    overtime   46
  disabled workers   58-9
  exclusions   50-2
    "Act of God" provisions   52
    different places of work
      distance apart   50-1
    domestic service   52
    need for continuity of service   51
    place of work and place of
      residence distance apart   50-1
    special cases   50-2
    surge of activity   51-2
    work involving special hazards
      or heavy physical or mental
      strain   52-3
  health assessments   56-7
    young workers   72-3
  health problems, transfer
    to day work   57-8
  maintaining records   56

medical conditions which increase
  risk to individual by working
  at night   57
normal working hours   45-9
overtime, compulsory   48
pregnant workers   14
reference period   48-50
  calculating average hours
    of work   49, 96
  compulsory overtime   48
  new workers   48
  rolling   48
rest breaks, monotonous work   53
shift patterns   54-6
  12-hour rotating   44, 55
  eight-hour shifts (Mon - Fri)
    and two 12-hour shifts on
    one in three weekends   55
  rotating continental
    eight-hour pattern   44-5, 54-5
night-work limits, enforcement   84
Northern Ireland   1
nuclear installations   84

offices   84
on-call time   17, 18, 33
opt-out of 48-hour working
  week   13, 14, 21, 26-8
  agreements   26
    cut-off date   26
  consideration required before
    requesting   27
  existing workers   27-8
  new workers   26-7
  record-keeping   27, 28
  workers with more than
    one job   28
opt-out agreements
  overtime   96
  variation of rest period
    entitlements   40
overtime
  night workers   46, 48
  opt-out agreements   96
  voluntary   24, 28
    calculation of 48-hour
      average   24

part-time workers, holiday entitlement	66-7
police service	6, 8
postal services	22, 23, 38, 51
pregnant workers	
night work	14
risk assessment	60
press	22, 38, 51
prisons	22, 38, 51
pub workers	44
public holidays	67
publication of Regulations	4
quarries	84
R v Attorney General for Northern Ireland ex parte Burns	45
radio	22, 38, 51
railway workers	2, 7
re-engagement, definition	91
record keeping, 48-hour working week	28-30
inspection of records	28
monitoring hours worked	29
opt-out agreement	27, 28
retention of records	28, 29
reinstatement, definition	91
relevant agreements	32
definition	10
holiday entitlement	65
night time hours	43-4
religious ceremonies, workers officiating at	16, 37, 50
remedies for breach of provisions *see* breach of provisions; employment tribunal complaints	
research and development activities	22, 38, 51
residential institutions	22, 38, 51
rest periods	9, 31-41
agreements, benefits	34
compensatory rest	39
daily rest	31, 34, 86
night workers	46-7
definition	32
entitlements	31, 32
link with health and safety	31
payment for	36
rest breaks	18, 31, 35
employment tribunal complaints	86
monotonous work	35-6
enforcement	84-5
shift workers	39
special cases	37-9
unmeasured working time	36-7
variation of entitlements	40-1
collective and workforce agreements	40
compensatory rest	40-1
individual opt-out agreements	40
weekly rest	31, 34-5, 86
young workers *see under* young workers	
retail premises	84
retail staff working increased hours over Christmas and New Year	23
road workers	2, 7
sales representatives	37
school leaving age, minimum	71-2
schools	84
sea fishing	2, 7
sea, workers at	2, 7
security and surveillance activities	21, 38
self-employed	6
definition	14
shift length	34
shift patterns	
12-hour rotating	44, 55
eight-hour shifts (Mon - Fri) and two 12-hour shifts on one in three weekends	55
rotating continental eight hour pattern	44-5, 54-5
shift work, definition	39
shift workers	
definition	39
rest period	39
sick leave, calculation of 48-hour average	24
Sindicato de Médicos de Asistencia Pública (Simap) v Conselleria de Sanidad y Consuma de la	

Index 107

Generalidad Valenciana	33	workforce agreements	
sports	84	definition	10
standby	33	failure to sign	
state workers	5	unfair dismissal	88
surge of activity	22-3, 38	unlawful detriment	87
		night workers	53
tea breaks	34	requirements for valid	11-12
telecommunications services	22, 38, 51	rest period entitlements	40
		signature	11
television	22, 38, 51	to extend reference period	2-1, 23
temporary staff, measurement of 48-hour limit	20	workforce representatives	11-12
tourism	23, 38, 51	workforce representatives	
trainees, non-employed	6	unfair dismissal	88
transport sector	8	unlawful detriment	87
travel time	17	working time	
travel to and from different sites	33	activities considered as	33-4
		definition	9, 32
		young workers' limit	72
UK challenge to EC Directives	2-3	working time regulations	
ECJ ruling	3	consent form	101
unfair dismissal, worker's form of redress	87, 89	workplace distance from home	21, 50-1
unfair dismissal (employees)	87, 88-9	workplace layout, young workers	73
armed forces, redress procedures	89	workplaces distant from one another	21, 50-1
qualifying period	89	written contract of employment	10
qualifying reasons	88		
remedies	90-3		
basic award	92-3	Young Persons (Scotland) Act 1937	78
compensatory award	93	young workers	71-9
re-engagement	91-2	48-hour week	72
reinstatement	91	agricultural work	78
see also under employment tribunal complaints		annual leave	77
unmeasured working time		Children (Protection at Work) Regulations 1998	71, 78-9
48-hour working week	15-16	compensatory rest, employment tribunal complaints	86
rest periods	36-7	definition	7, 71
water industry	22, 38, 51	exposure to physical, biological or chemical agents	74, 75
weekly rest	31, 34-5	exposure to radiation	75
employment tribunal complaints	86	health assessment	73-4
work equipment, use by young workers	73-4	night work	72-3
worker, definition	5-6, 14	health and safety training	74
workers with more than one job	25-6, 28, 76-7	Health and Safety (Young Persons) Regulations 1997	71, 73-5

light work 78
night work 72-3
paid public performances -
  local authority licence 79
performing abroad 79
rest periods 32, 75-7, 78
  conditions necessary for
    modification or exclusion 77
  minimum weekly 76
  rest breaks 75, 76
  school holidays 78-9
  where employee has more
    than one job 76-7
risk assessments 74-5
ship work 71
training 75
use of work equipment 73-4
weekly working hour -
  maximum 78
working-time limit 72
workplace layout 73
Young Persons (Scotland)
  Act 1937 78